MOVING WITHIN THE CIRCLE

CONTEMPORARY NATIVE AMERICAN MUSIC AND DANCE

MOVING WITHIN THE CIRCLE

CONTEMPORARY NATIVE AMERICAN MUSIC AND DANCE

BRYAN BURTON
WEST CHESTER UNIVERSITY

WORLD MUSIC PRESS

MOVING WITHIN THE CIRCLE:
CONTEMPORARY NATIVE AMERICAN MUSIC AND DANCE
by
Bryan Burton

Published by:
World Music Press
Judith Cook Tucker, Publisher; Editor-in-Chief
PO Box 2565 Danbury CT 06813-2565 (203) 748-1131

ISBN 0-937203-41-6 Book
ISBN 0-937203-43-2 Book/audio tape SET
ISBN 0-937203-50-5 Book/audio tape/slides SET

Original Paperback Edition
Printed in the United States of America by BookCrafters on recycled, acid-free paper.
2 3 4 5 6

Music engraved by Don Wallace using Music Prose®.
Book and cover design by Claudia Chapman.

Thank you to all who pulled together to make this project possible.
Your generosity of spirit will not be forgotten.

Library of Congress Card Catalog Number
LC 93-1578

Library of Congress Cataloging-in-Publication Data

Burton, Bryan, 1948-
    Moving within the circle: contemporary native American music and
dance/Bryan Burton.-- Original pbk. ed.
        p.   cm.
    Includes melodies and words to twenty-five songs, flute pieces,
and dances.
    Discography: p.
    Includes bibliographical references and index.
    1. Indians of North America—Music. 2. Indians of North America-
-Dances. 3. Folk music--United States. 4. Folk dancing--United
States.   I. Title.
ML3557.B8 1993
781.62'97--dc20
                                        93-1578
                                        MN

ABOUT THE AUTHOR

BRYAN BURTON

Bryan Burton, Associate Professor of Music Education at West Chester University of Pennsylvania, holds bachelor's, master's, and doctoral degrees from West Texas State University, Western State College of Colorado, and the University of Southern Mississippi, respectively. His interest in multicultural music has taken him as both researcher and lecturer to China, Japan, Korea, Hong Kong, Great Britain, Mexico, the Caribbean, and numerous Native American Nations within the United States and Canada. Dr. Burton has served as clinician, adjudicator, and guest conductor in eighteen states as well. Prior to joining West Chester, he served on the faculty of Frostburg State University (Maryland) and taught music at the public school level for fourteen years. His articles have appeared in numerous journals and he is the author of *Ceremonial and Social Songs and Dances of Selected Native Peoples of the Southwestern United States* and *Artisans of the American Southwest*. Of mixed Native American and European descent, his long-standing interest in the music of the original inhabitants of North America has led him to meet and work with many fine musicians, and he has shared their social dances and songs with music teachers at state, national and in-service presentations. He is a member of the Music Educators National Conference, National Band Association, College Band Directors National Association, College Music Society, Alpha Chi Honor Society, Phi Mu Alpha Sinfonia, and is an honorary member of Kappa Kappa Psi.

ACKNOWLEDGMENTS

The Lakota proverb "whoever makes decisions alone is not making good decisions," certainly applies to the creation of a book. Any text such as this is the product of many hands, voices and eyes. The greatest debt owed is to those Native Americans both cited in the text and those wishing to remain unnamed for their guidance during my study of these songs, dances and traditions.

A great debt is owed to the staff members of cultural museums, tribal museums and associations, both large and small, who were so generous with their time and knowledge, and of course the staff at Canyon Records.

I'd also like to thank my long-suffering students for serving as guinea-pigs during the preparation of this text, and to those teachers around the world who have tried out the materials in classroom settings.

Thank you to David McAllester for his thoughtful comments in reviewing the final manuscript.

Thanks especially to Ebby my cat, who occasionally would deign to allow me to get up out of the recliner, out from under her, and work on the manuscript.

And thank you to all those people who in many capacities have helped to nurture this project.

CONTENTS

About the Author, v
List of Musical Transcriptions, 3
List of Photographs and Illustrations, 4
Preface, 5
Map, 8
Terminology: The Debate Continues, 9

1 ENTERING THE CIRCLE: LEARNING TO LEARN, 11
A Personal Odyssey

2 SHAPING THE SOUND: STYLE, FORM, SUBSTANCE, 19
Concept and Function • Vocables• Regional Styles
Instruments: Voices of the Circle
Strings • Drums • Rattles • Other Percussion • Flutes

3 UNITING THE CIRCLES: THE INTERTRIBAL POW-WOW, 33
Dance types: Grand Entry • Flag Song • Men's Traditional Dance • Women's
Traditional Dance • Men's Fancy War Dance • Fancy Shawl Dance • Grass
Dance • Jingle Dance • Hoop Dance • Eagle Dance • Intertribal Social Dances
• Attending a Pow-wow

4 MOVING WITHIN THE CIRCLE: SONGS AND DANCES, 41
Privacy and Usage • Lyrics or Vocables • Notation and Pronunciation • Variants
Songs and Dances:
  "Song to the Four Directions" (Alabama-Coushatta), 48
  "I Walk in Beauty" (Navajo/Apache Friendship Dance), 50
  "Canoe Song" (Haliwa-Saponi), 54
  "Bear Dance" (Haliwa-Saponi), 57
  Introduction to Round Dances, 61
  "Pueblo Round Dance," 64
  "Intertribal Dance," 66
  "Pottery Dance" (Zuni), 68
  "Basket Dance" (Pueblo Ysleta del Sur), 70
  "Nanticoke Shawl Dance," 73
  "Pueblo Two-Step," 77
  "Rabbit Dance" (Flute version, South Dakota), 82
  "Rabbit Dance" (Vocal version: Seneca), 82
  "One-Eyed Ford" (Intertribal), 85

5 SONGS OF THE WIND: THE NATIVE AMERICAN FLUTE, 87

Legend: Origin of the Indian Love Flute
Legend: The Story of the Woodpecker Flute, 90
Legend: The Story of the Orphan Boy, 91
Playing the Native American flute, 92
Listen and absorb the style, 93
    "Pueblo Flute Song" (Zuni), 94
    "Call to Sunrise" (Zuni), 95
    "Lakota Courting Song," 96
    "Kiowa Love Song," 97
    "Hidatsa Dance Song," 98

6 A MYRIAD OF VOICES: GUIDED LISTENING EXPERIENCES, 99

Introduction, 101
    "Picture Song," 102
    "Cuero Mohelam," 104
    "...Then there was Wood," 107
    "Zuni Sunrise Song," 108
    "I'm Happy About You," 110
    Ghost Dance, 113

7 MAKING INSTRUMENTS THE NEW OLD-FASHIONED WAY, 117

Dance Jingles: Traditional • Contemporary, 121
Wrist/Ankle Bells, 124
Recycled Rattle, 125
Gourd Rattle, 127
Drum Beaters: Navajo • Apache • Generic, 129
Rasps: Yaqui-style rasp • Bear Dance style rasp, 132
Drums: Log drums • Water drums • Hand drums, 134

8 APPENDIX, 139

Where to Find More Information about the Tribes Included or Cited in this
Resource, 140
When Visiting a Reservation, 141
Chief Seattle's Speech, 142
Discography, 145
Bibliography, 155
Videos, 159
Instrument makers • Craft supplies • Cultural centers • Other resources 161
Index, 165

LIST OF MUSICAL TRANSCRIPTIONS

"Song to the Four Directions" (Alabama-Coushatta), 48

"I Walk in Beauty" (Navajo/Apache Friendship Dance), 50

"Canoe Song" (Haliwa-Saponi), 54

"Bear Dance" (Haliwa-Saponi), 59

"Pueblo Round Dance," 64

"Intertribal Dance," 66

"Pottery Dance" (Zuni), 68

"Basket Dance" (Pueblo Ysleta del Sur), 70

"Nanticoke Shawl Dance," 74

"Pueblo Two-Step," 80

"Rabbit Dance (Flute version)," 82

"Rabbit Dance" (vocal version) (Seneca), 82

"One-Eyed Ford" (Intertribal), 86

"Pueblo Sunrise Song" (Zuni), 94

"Call to Sunrise" (Zuni), 95

"Lakota Courting Song," 96

"Kiowa Love Song," 97

"Hidatsa Dance Song," 98

LIST OF PHOTOGRAPHS AND ILLUSTRATIONS

Dedicated young dancer, Gallup, New Mexico, 1986 (photo: John Running), cover
Bryan Burton (photo: Gerry Burton), v
Map of the United States (artist: Claudia Chapman), 8
An elder of the Blood Tribe, Stand Off, Alberta, Canada (photo: Running), 11
Plains design Medicine Wheel (photo: Bryan Burton), 17
Crow Fair, Montana, 1992 (photo: Running), 19
Apache violin (artist: C. Chapman), 26
Taos drum (photo: B. Burton), 26
Tarahumara Drum (photo: B. Burton), 27
Water Drum from Six Nations Reserve (photo: B. Burton), 27
Drums and Rattles:
    Micmac drum; Tuscarora drum; Cochiti drum; Ute Rawhide rattle; Cherokee tortoise
    shell rattle, Iroquois horn rattle, Tigua gourd rattle, contemporary gourd rattles (all
    photos: B. Burton), 28
Hopi Owl Kachina Rattle (photo: B. Burton), 29
Flutes: Kiowa, Apache, Cheyenne, Carter, Bear MacFarlane Flute (photos: B. Burton), 30
Living With Tradition:
    Ruby Olson, Haliwa-Saponi, in jingle dress; Acoma Intercultural Dancers drummers;
    Berni Keyope performing social dance; Alden Keyope performing Buffalo Dance (all
    photos: B. Burton), 32
The Drum at a Cherokee pow-wow, 1991 (photo: Running), 33
(Top): Anthony Dean Stanton and Richard Wilcox in Narragansett Regalia(C.Chapman), 40
(Bottom): Paul Roaring Winds dancing Sneak-up (C. Chapman), 40
Little Shell Pow-Wow Dancers, Ft. Berthold, North Dakota, 1986 (photo: Running), 41
Paul Roaring Winds wearing bear claw (C. Chapman), 59
Young Pueblo dancers (photo: B. Burton), 65
Haliwa-Saponi Dancers (photo: B. Burton), 67
Zuni Pottery dancers (pen and ink: C. Chapman, after a photo by Bryan Burton), 68
Nanticoke Shawl dancers (pen and ink: C. Chapman), 74
Two-Step, as danced by the Haliwa-Saponi Dancers (photo: B. Burton), 81
R. Carlos Nakai, flutist and educator (photo: Running), 87
Native American flute (pen and ink: Phyllis Tarlow), 89
Diagram and detail of Native American flutes (photo: B. Burton; drawing: C. Chapman), 92
The Drum at a Gathering, Ft. Hall, Idaho: The Recording Studio (photo: Running), 99
The Porcupine Singers (Canyon Records Production), 102
Glafiro "Papos" Perez, a Yaqui Deer Dancer (photo: Terry Hollinger), 104
Jackalope (photo: Gordon Fong), 106
Pueblo Village at Laguna (photo: B. Burton), 108
XIT (photo: Far West Photography), 110
Tatanka-Ptecila (Short Bull) c. 1904 (photo: Natalie Curtis), 113
Handmade drums at Santa Clara Pueblo, New Mexico (photo: Running), 117
Making jingles (diagrams by C. Chapman), 121-122
Making contemporary jingles (photos: B. Burton), 123
Wrist/ankle bells (drawing: C. Chapman), 124
Recycled rattle instructions (drawings: C. Chapman), 125-126
Gourd Rattle instructions (drawings: C. Chapman), 127-128
Drum beaters (pen and ink: C. Chapman), 129-131
Yaqui rasp (photo: B. Burton), 132
(L-R): Bear dance style rasp, Yaqui style rasp (photo: Judith Cook Tucker), 133
Log drum (photo: B. Burton), 135
Water drums: top: Navajo pottery bean pot; bottom: carved wood from Six Nations Reserve,
    Ontario, Canada (Photos: B. Burton), 136

PREFACE

During the past decade, there has been an expansive rebirth of interest in all things Native American. From movies to television advertisements to art to music, Native American or Native American inspired topics daily enter our awareness.

The awe-inspiring grandeur of Monument Valley (*The Land of Long Shadows* to the Navajo), long a staple in John Ford westerns, has become a favorite backdrop for advertising: a typist perches precariously atop the "Totem Pole" formation touting an IBM typewriter; four-wheel drive vehicles compete in contrasting commercials featuring drives to mesa tops; a battery operated bunny pounds away on a bass drum while traversing an isolated highway. Madison Avenue has used the voice of Navajo musician D.J. Nez in an automobile commercial to persuade the audience of the realism of the stereo system when a rainstorm is supposedly brought about from a taped song.

Native Americans are at last receiving balanced or sympathetic portrayals in major motion pictures including: *Black Robe*, the story of French missionaries in seventeenth century Canada; *Last of His Tribe*, the true story of Ishi, the lone survivor of a California tribe; *Last of the Mohicans*; *Thunderheart* featuring a Native American detective, and the Academy Award-winning *Dances With Wolves*. The producers of several of these films employed numerous Native American craftspeople to create clothing, weapons, daily tools, and housing for increased realism. Native American actors were used for Native roles, and in *Dances with Wolves* the Lakota language was used for dialogue, and a respected musical group (the Porcupine Singers) provided traditional music for several scenes. Plans are underway for the production of more films featuring major roles for Native Americans including one of Tony Hillerman's Jim Chee mysteries.

Native American influences have, indeed, strongly entered mainstream commercial sales. Specialty stores featuring "Southwestern" designs and mail order catalogs offering everything from Native American (and Native American inspired) jewelry to mandalas and dance costumes are now a staple of our trendy society. The unavoidable "Santa Fe Style" is found in major retail lines and catalogs. "New Age" music, philosophy, and design reveal a significant debt to Native America.

Interest in Native Americana has taken an even more

personal turn: more people are now claiming real or imagined "Indian" ancestors prompting one Native American to comment that "the Wannabes are now the largest tribe in the country." In truth, many "white" Americans may have Native American ancestors. However, such "impurities" were often hidden in family genealogies assigning these darker branches of the family tree to such groups as "Black Dutch," "Black Irish," or "Mediterranean." In cases where the ancestry was not hidden, Native Americans were often promoted to the status of "Indian Princess" or "King of the Cherokees." Because of such practices, the true identity of the individuals and tribes were often lost to present-day generations seeking accurate genealogies.* This Native American renaissance has created an opportunity for us to study the original American culture, its structure, beliefs, music.

The search for "authenticity" in Native American music has been hampered by several factors: (1) the total elimination of numerous tribal cultures; (2) concerted efforts by missionaries and early settlers to "civilize" Indians and eliminate "paganistic" dances and songs; (3) distrust of white scholars by Native Americans (even today, there is a what might be called a "BS factor" in evaluating information given to non-native Americans regarding ceremonial aspects of music); (4) the inordinately long delay in recognizing the value of the Native American culture. In short, many Native American music and dance traditions have been irretrievably lost.

Fortunately, there were a few researchers who valued the Native American culture and actively sought to preserve the music and dance. Beginning with the early cylinder recordings of Jesse Walter Fewkes and Frances Densmore, the early transcriptions of songs and stories by Natalie Curtis, and continuing to the work of David McAllester and Willard Rhodes, there have been sensitive scholars seeking to preserve the musical culture of the Native American. The Cylinder Project at the Folk Life Center of the Library of Congress has given back copies of the oldest and rarest recordings to the people for whom they are of critical importance. Louis Ballard's *American Indian Music for the Classroom* and Lynn Huenemann's *Songs and Dances of Native America* (both currently out of print) offered music educators, reservation schools and outreach programs a body of songs and dances that were authentic, accessible, and buttressed by cultural context.

To meet the demand for information about the first Americans, publishers have begun to reissue older texts (some dating back to the early Nineteenth century), including the Densmore and Curtis studies of Native American music, and publish newer works providing a more contemporary perspective. General music basal series are including more authentic Native American songs and dances often provided by Native American musicians and scholars

---

*(The author's family sometimes jokes they are descended from the *"that"* tribe...as in, *"That* Indian your great-great grandfather married." Other families refer to their tribe as "those"...as in, *"Those* Oklahoma Indians your family married into.")

and are eliminating inappropriate sacred songs as well as spurious songs previously passed as "Indian." Interest in Native American music has created a thriving market in recordings by Native musicians, frequently produced by Native American owned companies such as Canyon Records, or those with strong ties to the Native American community, such as Indian House. Given the resurgence of interest and renewed availability of materials, what can we learn from the Native Americans, whether the lesson is about our own roots and branches, as in my family, or whether it is of ancient peoples and cultures with traditions of universal value?

We can learn how this culture survived an intense campaign to eradicate all elements of Native society. Governmental edicts dating from the 1880s sought to break down the culture through bans on language, religion, and music. Native children were sent away to boarding schools to destroy links with their past. The only legal performances of Native American music for nearly an entire generation were for theatrical purposes (Buffalo Bill's "Wild West Show," for example) and for tourist groups near reservations such as performances at the Grand Canyon or for the Santa Fe Railroad's special travel concessions.

We can learn how this culture continued to grow and thrive despite these efforts at destruction. "Illegal" performances, ceremonies, and language, of course, continued as elders sought to pass on traditional values and knowledge to the younger generations, secretly if necessary. Some examples exist where, outwardly, dances adopted "white" formats, yet retained Native meanings and functions. An oral tradition can never be eliminated through edict.

We can learn how this culture—now free of the onerous restrictions—has blossomed into a dynamic part of contemporary American life. Native American music now encompasses a full range from traditional music to jazz-influenced, classical, rock, country, popular, and "New Age" styles.

Perhaps the important lessons we can learn from the Native American include how much we have lost in our overly specialized society through assigning music to professionals rather than "the people," how important music can be to the cycles of individual and community life, how we may yet be able to recover our own musical heritage, and a process for the study and preservation of music from all ethnic elements in our American mosaic.

LOCATION OF TRIBES WHOSE MEMBERS
HAVE CONTRIBUTED IN SOME WAY
TO THE CREATION OF THIS PROJECT

Micmac
Tuscarora
Mohawk
Seneca

Nanticoke
Haliwa-Saponi
Lumbee

Cherokee

Cheyenne
Hidatsa
Crow
Lakota

Kiowa

Alabama-Coushatta

Ute
Taos
Cochiti
Zuni
Acoma

Tigua

Navajo
Yavapai
Apache
Yaqui

Tarahumara

Tohono O'Odham

TERMINOLOGY
THE DEBATE CONTINUES

Indians
Native Americans
None of the Above

Choosing a term to apply to those peoples whose ancestors occupied the western continents prior to 1492 is not an easy task. Each term in current usage has some degree of invalidity from cultural, historical, or political viewpoints.

Columbus, thinking he had reached the Indies, called those who greeted him "Indios," a term we now consider as not only inaccurate, but insensitive. In parts of Latin America, the term "Indios" referring to native populations is considered a racial epithet and use of the term may result in fines or other punishment. (Peter Matthiessen suggests that the term *indios* may, in fact, be a corruption of the term *una gente in dios*—a people in God—a reference to the idyllic lifestyle of the first peoples encountered by Columbus.)

The term "Indian" used in the United States carries much racist and prejudicial baggage from the period of westward expansion bringing to mind General Philip Sheridan's comment "The only good Indian I ever saw was dead," often quoted as "The only good Indian is a dead Indian." Generations of children playing "cowboys and Indians" always assigned the undesirable role of Indian to the least desirable children and consistently slaughtered the "savages." References to "wild Indians" continue to be heard in admonitions for more socially acceptable behavior as in, "Quit acting like a wild Indian," even in public schools at all levels!

"Native Americans" is also a misnomer. The term "America" is European in origin—the continents were named for an Italian mapmaker and explorer—and was not used until the sixteenth century. (A frequently told story has a native speaker answering the question, "What was this country called before Columbus landed?" with the simple, "Ours!") Prior to the American Revolution, the term "American" was used almost exclusively in reference to native peoples rather than to the colonists.

References to "aboriginal" or "indigenous" peoples often carry a connotation of inferiority of culture. Even referring to a group as a "tribe" is viewed as deprecatory by some, who prefer the term "nation." In Canada, however, "Aboriginal People" is a term accepted by many groups as the preferred generic reference. "First People," "First Americans," "Original Americans," or "First Nations" are terms growing in popularity at present.

Too often, the encroaching white settlers used terms for tribes which were derogatory terms applied by other groups: i.e. "Apache" was a Zuni term for "Enemy of My People," "Sioux" was the ending of the word *Nadowessioux*, which originally was an Algonquian term defying decent translation but kindly interpreted as "deceitful snakes." Other labels were equally inaccurate: i.e. "Pueblo" referred to the style of dwelling; "Crow" was a mistranslation of hand signals that meant "Children of the Long-beaked Bird."

What did these people call themselves? Most identified their group with a term in their own language which meant simply "the people." Usually, some type of descriptive was added to distinguish groups: i.e. "Lenni Lenape" (Delaware) means "Original People," "Tohono O'odham" (Papago) means "People of the Desert." In the film *Little Big Man,* "Sioux" (Lakota) referred to themselves as "Real Human Beings," however "Dakota" or "Lakota" means "allied" or "many in one." The Navajo are "Dine(h)"—"people." (Many groups are now seeking to return to their original names in government documents and maps.)

In this resource, peoples will be identified by tribal affiliation where individuals or individual groups are discussed. "Native American" will be used as a generic term for general discussions or when more specific identification is, for some reason, undesirable. "Indian" will be used in historical contexts, direct quotations, formal song titles, and in some instances where repetition of "Native American" throughout a sentence or paragraph is grammatically awkward.

The use of such terminology is not to imply disrespect for any peoples. I have nothing but the deepest respect and love for the original peoples of our land, their culture and traditions.

CHAPTER **1**

LEARNING TO LEARN · ENTERING THE CIRCLE

Photo on the previous page: An elder of the Blood Tribe,
Stand Off, Alberta, Canada. The wisdom of his own years
is added to the wisdom of his people, passed along via
stories that teach, and insights shared with the true Learner.
(Photo: John Running © 1986)

LEARNING TO LEARN
ENTERING THE CIRCLE

RESEARCH IN THE ORAL TRADITION

A personal odyssey

This collection is not meant to be definitive, or even particularly comprehensive. Given the existence of some three hundred federally recognized tribes in the United States, and more than one hundred and fifty groups not officially recognized, this can only serve as a beginning. Nothing was included that was not taught to me directly, and so there are culture areas with equally rich traditions that are not represented in these pages. It is simply a peek into the musical and cultural pockets and backpack of one man, myself, as he was nurtured by many musicians who saw he was ready to learn what they were ready to offer.

"Learning" is a more accurate description than "research" of the process used in gathering materials for this book. "Research" often carries the implication of a totally detached, formally structured style of investigation which is inappropriate for those who wish to immerse themselves in the total humanity of the Native American peoples.

How can one remain formally detached when sharing a meal with a family in their hogan somewhere on the Navajo reservation, watching their children play, seeing the mother weaving intricate designs without using a pattern, helping the father and sons move sheep to a new pasturing site? Is it possible to isolate oneself from the deep love and respect the Native American shows for Mother Earth? Can the investigator remain untouched by timeless rituals performed to bring rain to desert fields? Does the observer ignore the feelings shown by a master carver or potter singing a "special" song while creating her works?

A Learner becomes a part of the experience. A Learner "becomes" part of the people from whom he or she learns. The songs, dances, stories, and history in this book were learned from Native Americans the old-fashioned way—through an oral tradition of passing the information from person to person and learning by doing. The process may appear slow to another casual observer, but the richness of experience obliterates any sense of time in the western sense.

Learning from the Native American peoples almost never takes place in a formal setting. Songs were often learned from performers at pow-wows, dances, and fairs during breaks between competitions and performances. One song was learned while bouncing through Monument Valley in the back of an ageless pick-up truck of unidentifiable origin accompanying a singer whose primary source of income was guiding tourists through the area. Other materials were learned in settings including a picnic ground, hotel lobby, parking lot in front of a supermarket, and sheep pasture. From these experiences, the Learner discovers that music is pervasive in Native American cultures and is not restricted to formal presentations by trained professionals. The importance of music to these first Americans only underscores the extent to which so much of non-Indian America has lost its folk music culture.

Learning from Native Americans requires overcoming a number of obstacles. Secrecy is one of the most difficult barriers to penetrate. Secrecy is used to control knowledge about the culture which should be restricted to its initiated members. Some tribal members fear that their knowledge will lose its power if openly discussed with outsiders. Observations of Native Americans are filled with examples of "polite evasiveness" as a technique for cultural survival.

One must overcome many centuries of distrust in order to learn from this culture. The process of gaining trust and confidence is ongoing and the method varies with each individual. Most often, patience and more patience are the key to success. In the past, graduate students seeking dissertation data have descended upon tribes seeking fast answers to their questions and ignoring tribal requests for confidentiality. The worst of these have persuaded people to divulge privileged information under promises of complete discretion, only to rush into publication exposing rituals or other information while failing to guard against protecting the identity of sources. The sources must remain and face the consequences of this indiscretion from other tribal members. On occasion, persistent questioners have been given disinformation just to quiet them or to cause them to appear foolish.

Learners realize the importance of respecting the wishes of those willing to teach. Literature by such individuals reveals only that which is permitted by the source and the identity of the source is given only with the express permission of that individual. In this book, some songs have been given vocables or a different set of vocables to meet such restrictions. Identities of sources have been guarded when requested.

Native America holds the same range of individual views—ultra-conservative to liberal—regarding cultural beliefs as any society. Some individuals view any revelation as "blasphemy" while others discuss all matters quite freely. However, it is often necessary to obscure the purpose of talking to an outsider to avoid criticism from conservative members of the community.

These beliefs influenced the process of learning the materials in this book. In one instance, I spent an entire day following a person from trading post to trading post while his wife sold blankets and he worked on jewelry. While the individual was, indeed, customizing a jewelry order for me, he was also singing songs and telling old children's tales for my benefit. In another case, the leader of a music troupe told me that although I could not tape and photograph a performance in the village, I was welcome to come with them to a nearby fair where the performance would be considered "theatrical" rather than "ritual" and, therefore, could be recorded. Over the years, I have become friends with a number of groups performing on the "pow-wow circuit" and am almost expected to be at events to learn more. It is not uncommon to hear, "Hey! We're looking for you—we've got a great dance step to show you."

Another obstacle to overcome in learning Native American musics is that this is an oral tradition and the music, obviously, is not restricted to those performance conventions easily notated in western art notation. Songs sometimes must be notated to the nearest equivalent. Because of this oral transmission of information, the same song may vary extremely from group to group. Individual tastes and tribal or clan preferences will be reflected in versions of a song. Also, performance of the same song by the same group may vary between performances. Native American music is in a state of constant evolution. Nothing is carved in stone. It is possible to learn two versions of one social dance song on different sides of the same highway!

The songs and dances in this text have been transcribed as faithfully as possible while keeping the notation within the reach of the general music classroom student. Rhythms and pitches may sound slightly different, in some cases, on original tapes and the notated version due to difficulties of transcribing music from an oral tradition. Vocables used for some of the transcriptions have been adjusted slightly to avoid difficulty of pronouncing sounds for which the English language does not have equivalent. All materials have been taken back to Native sources for comment and suggestions following the initial transcription. Following any further revisions, the materials were tested in classrooms at all levels, kindergarten to university, and in locales from New England to Singapore. The result, hopefully, is a set of usable materials for the study of contemporary Native American musics by students of all ages.

Finally, learning the materials for this book has been part of a personal odyssey for me. A case could be made for a starting date for this odyssey as being 1736 when an earlier Burton reportedly abandoned his farm in Georgia and "went to the Carolinas and there dwelt among the Indians." Since that time, roots of the family tree have extended into both cultures although the "white" ancestors usually failed to specify tribe or original name of individuals from the "redder" blossoms on the tree.

From 1817 to about 1863, another ancestor, Jacob Wolf, assumed the position of government agent for the Cherokee, Shawnee and Choctaw, located (and "relocated" with the Cherokee "Trail of Tears") in northern Arkansas. He had moved from North Carolina to Arkansas, and built a house on the edge of the reservation. (The family home is now a state museum and park.) Trained as a carpenter, he taught carpentry to the Cherokee and helped to build houses. When the Civil War broke out, the government confiscated his property, and he died soon after. He was buried with honor by the Cherokee, (who called him "The Great Father of the North Fork,") on what was Cherokee Reservation land. Although no clear evidence of intermarriage occurs in this family line, a close affinity with Native American customs, including recipes that clearly have their roots in indigenous cuisine, entered the family consciousness.

The Native American ancestor from the mid-nineteenth century is a woman whose specific tribal identity has proved elusive. Enough evidence exists, however, to persuade the genealogist to promote this woman to "Cherokee Princess." (After all, the reasoning in the old records seems to follow, if a good old Southern family accepted her, she *must* be royalty. Many persons of mixed heritage have been told they had a "princess" in their family tree, however the Cherokee were, and are, a democratic tribe, and titles of royalty are not used, and are not relevant or appropriate.) Cherokee? It is possible—a sizable group of Cherokee did settle between the Sabine and Trinity rivers in East Texas in the early nineteenth century and this was also the locale of the family homestead. However, early family letters indicate she was Caddo (a people also known as Tejas who tended to be fairly light-skinned and friendly to the white settlers who arrived in their territory).

Then came the mid-twentieth century when I accompanied my journalist mother to interviews with surviving pioneer families of the plains of West Texas. These interviewees had settled in an area opened only in the late nineteenth century following the end of the wars against the Comanche and had vivid memories of seeing isolated "wild Indians" still living a nomadic life and occasionally begging at the kitchen door to supplement their hunting. Artifacts literally littered the ground throughout my home region; pictographs and other signs struggled to survive target practice of young farm boys; old campsites held pottery shards, dolls, and flint tools.

Other families remembered stories from their parents concerning building homes under threat of attack and of dealings with prominent Comanche leaders such as Quanah Parker (who later became a leading businessman, rancher, and religious leader). Among neighbors was an old cowhand who had served as cook on cattle drives. (My grandmother recalled moving from east Texas to New Mexico Territory in a covered wagon and experienced cattle stampedes and other pioneering events.)

The interest sparked by these stories has never died.

In all Native American cultures, the image of the circle may be found again and again. It is found in the dances, the arts, the shape of the lodgings. The circle, however, is more than an artistic or architectural device: the circle is the basis of all Native American beliefs. Everything is connected to everything else with all people, nature, and the Creator being part of this universal circle. Wherever one goes, and whoever one becomes, one remains part of all existence and must seek to maintain that balance in nature which the Navajo call "Hozho"—Beauty. When one walks in Beauty, one is in harmony with the universe and is moving within the Circle.

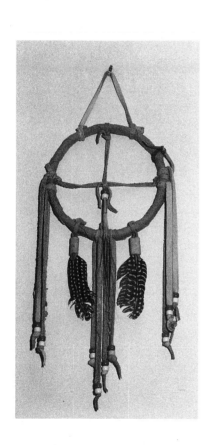

The personal circle which began more than two centuries ago has resulted in this offering of songs, dances, stories, history, and photographs. Since 1978, under the tutelage of many guides, I have set foot a step at a time to uncover and rediscover the journey my ancestors took, with the music as my vehicle—a journey which continues over the months and years as I seek more teachers who might assist this exploration and nurturing of traditional culture within my contemporary self. Take this book and tape with their voices, their songs, and in some cases, their images—these things they were willing to offer to you and to their own children who will use this volume in their community centers, in the hopes of increasing understanding of the immense value of their ways. This brief meeting is only a starting point, a gateway through which you may enter into the music that unites the ever-spiraling circles of friendship, relationships with the earth, animals and people, cycles of the seasons, and life passages. Move within the circles, with respect for these ancient traditions that still resonate vibrantly throughout the Americas, in a spirit of harmony and true community.

THE "TRAIL OF TEARS"
An era, not an isolated event

Most non-Indians associate the "Trail of Tears" with the final 1838 removal of the last of the so-called Five Civilized Tribes (the Cherokee, Choctaw, Chickasaw, Creek and Seminole) from the southeastern United States to Indian Territory west of the Mississippi River. However, the actual tribal histories consider the entire period of removal as dating from the 1790s to the entire decade before the Civil War and includes both voluntary and forced removals. Voluntary removal was chosen by many of the more traditional tribal members who felt compelled to move away from encroaching white settlements. They migrated by the beginning of the 19th century to parts of what is now Missouri, Arkansas, Kansas and Oklahoma. (These areas were not yet part of the United States.) As a result, the Cherokee presence in what is now Oklahoma was significant enough by 1800 to allow formation of local schools, and in 1818 a representative tribal governing body enacted a public school law for the Cherokee establishing curriculum and structure of the educational system and employing Sequoyah (inventor of the Cherokee alphabet) to supervise education for the tribe.

Forced removal peaked during the Jackson administration, from 1828-1837. Methods varied, from riding on horseback dragging household and family possessions behind, to walking on harsh overland trails escorted by the U.S. military, to sailing on steamers around the gulf of Mexico, entering Texas through Galveston, or moving up the Mississippi River from New Orleans. Traumatic removals affected the Choctaw (nearly a quarter died during the bitterly cold journey); the Creeks, many of whom were marched in chains out of Alabama at gunpoint (almost 3,500 died on their journey); the Chicasaws, moved out of Tennessee in 1837 and who were overcome by cholera; the Cherokees, 18,000 of whom were forced out of Georgia by the U.S. Army in 1838 and made to walk 800 miles to Indian Territory (4,000 died en route). Some Cherokee were able to escape and made their way into the mountains of North Carolina, where their descendants may still be found. The Seminole kept up their resistance in the swamp lands of Florida, pursued by government troops until only a few hundred remained at the official conclusion of the Seminole War (1842). However, small bands continued to resist for several years more, until, in 1858, the last chief of the Seminole agreed to move west of the Mississippi River, leaving only a few to struggle for survival protected by their knowledge of the swamps and thickets. This is but one illustration of the contradictions between official histories and the oral record of the Native people whose lives were so strongly affected by the arrival of the Europeans to the shores of this land.

CHAPTER **2**

SHAPING THE SOUND · STYLE, FORM, SUBSTANCE

Photo on the previous page: Ancient and modern co-exist
at the Crow Fair, Montana: teepees, trucks, and a fine horse
ready to greet old and new friends.
 (Photo: John Running © 1992)

STYLE, FORM, SUBSTANCE

MUSIC AND DANCE

Weaving the strands of rainbow wool

Native American musics are the only musics indigenous to the American continents. These musics come from a mosaic of cultures covering the western hemisphere. In North America alone, an estimated 300 languages were spoken prior to 1492. Religious beliefs ranging from animism to elaborate ceremonial theologies were developed by the Native peoples. Music and dance were and continue to be integral parts of these cultures from prehistoric times through the present.

Native American music within the borders of the United States (excluding Alaska) may be divided into six general stylistic regions: Eastern Woodlands, Plains, Great Basin and Plateau, Northwest Coast, California, and Southwest. However, within these general areas, there is further stylistic diversification by tribe, clan, or society. Also, during the years following the end of World War Two, an Inter-tribal style became widespread among Native Americans. Because of this multiplicity of styles, to speak of "Native American Music" as a single type of music is erroneous.

Many listeners identify as Native American music the "Indian" music of Hollywood motion pictures. For this music, studio composers created a stereotyped sound very loosely based on the style of Plains tribes. Unfortunately, this "style" was used for all tribes in movies regardless of tribal or regional authenticity. Confusion over tribal identity was frequently compounded by inaccurate geographic settings and use of non-Indian or incorrect tribal groups in these movies. For example, Monument Valley in the Navajo Nation has been used to represent locales as distant as Mexico and the Dakotas. Local Navajo have been "Apaches," "Cheyenne," "Sioux," etc. Tribal speech in these movies, although supposedly matching the "tribe," has usually been Navajo—several who have acted in the movies claim that some of the dialogue in "Indian" has been off-color jokes about the white actors!

CONCEPT AND FUNCTION

Native Americans consider music to be a gift from the Creator. All music is part of the Universe and individuals are allowed by the Creator to "catch" a song from this source. Music might be the product of an individual within a tribe or the result of a communal effort. Sometimes, the "composer" presents the song to a society and improvements/refinements are made as a group. Dance steps also are created either by individuals or by groups. Songs are considered as the property of an individual person, family, or tribe, although "rights" may be sold, traded, loaned, or given as a gift. These songs are passed to the next musician through oral transmission—few Native American songs were written down until transcribed by researchers. Recently, Native American composers such as Louis Ballard and Carlos Nakai have been composing and transcribing works for publication.

Generally, music among the Native Americans has been considered functional. Music serves to join the natural with the supernatural, the person with the Creator. Songs and dances contain spiritual powers which can help bring about a desired effect. The performers, both singers and dancers, serve to create the functional purpose of the music. (For example, among the Southwestern tribes, most rituals are directed toward bringing rain and sun at appropriate times to insure a good harvest. Correct performance of a cycle of rituals including singing, dancing, and chanting is considered essential to bring about this effect.)

Often, the performer is also responsible for the rituals associated with the song, with specific tasks or roles assigned to designated "assistants" from among the villagers. Certain types of songs are to be performed only by certain individuals: healing songs are to be performed by "medicine men"; songs associated with certain societies may only be performed by initiates of those societies. In most traditional cultures, the men were (and are) the principal singers; however, there is a large repertory of women's songs, and under certain circumstances women may sing any songs.

Functions served by music in Native American cultures included: (1) religious ceremonies (2) healing ceremonies; (3) work songs (4) game songs (5) songs to bring success in war, hunting, agriculture (6)"honoring" songs to recognize worthy individuals, including veterans (7) courting songs; (8) storytelling and (9) social songs and dances. Many songs honor animals in word, sound, and gesture. Bear dances, robin dances, fish dances—all have stylized steps, body posture and attitudes that create a strong sense of the animal's presence. Some of the dance regalia includes antlers, pelts, whole skins and feathered capes to enhance the impression that the animal is indeed present. Dancers and observers alike join in thanks and praise for the animals' gifts of warmth, food, shelter, useful tools or objects, or highly regarded personality traits.

VOCABLES

Language beyond place and time

When you listen to traditional or contemporary singing whether it is by Cherokee, Seneca, Haliwa-Saponi, Navajo or Tlingit singers, it is certain you will hear vocables featured prominently. Vocables are used by virtually all Native American groups. These are syllables—having no apparent meaning to the casual listener—which are sung throughout all or part of a song. "Wey yo hey," hey-ya yunga" and "gai yo wah" are examples of vocables. Vocables, however, may or may not have specific meaning to the performer or a specific "initiated" audience. In no case are they felt to be "silly sounds" or "nonsense syllables."A song may consist solely of vocables, solely of a linguistic text, or contain both text and vocables. In addition, once a song has been sung publicly, the vocables remain essentially the same for subsequent performances, in the same way that words with clearly defined meanings would not be changed randomly with every singing. In general, vocable sounds tend to match the vowel sounds or certain other characteristic sound combinations of the tribal language of the performer. Several theories have been advanced regarding the origin of vocables in Native American music, but none can be proven conclusively.

The two most common views are:

1. The song is a personal gift from the Creator and the words are known by, and important to, only the performer and Creator. Worshippers' utterances in many world traditions carry a similar meaning—the words and melodies convey the deepest expression of the heart and soul and do not require the trappings of formal language to communicate the content fully.

2. Vocables represent either the remnants or fragments of an archaic tribal language or may be an effort to imitate the sounds of the language of another tribe from which the song was obtained. In some cases, songs continued to be used by members of a tribe after their language became "extinct." Gradually, the correct pronunciation and specific word meanings were forgotten although the performers remembered the underlying content—"what the song was about"— and continued singing the "old words." Futher discussion of vocables is included in the introduction to songs and dances, "Moving Within the Circle: Lyrics."

23

REGIONAL STYLES

Tribes listed are examples, not entirety.

EASTERN WOODLANDS:

IROQUOIS · ALGONKIAN · OJIBWAY · CHOCTAW · CHEROKEE · DELAWARE · SAPONI · CADDO · PENOBSCOT · PEQUOT · NARRAGANSETT ·

1. Generally relaxed voices in medium and high range.
2. Vocal shake or pulsing at ends of phrases in particular;
3. Frequent use of call and response.
4. Agricultural themes, such as hunting and raising crops, are frequently used in lyrics.
5. Some use of song cycles.
6. Great variety of rhythmic accompaniments on drums, syncopation.
7. Instruments include small hand drums (some with water inside for increased resonance) and rattles made of turtle shells or cowhorn.

PLAINS:

DAKOTA · NAKOTA · LAKOTA (SIOUX) · KIOWA · COMANCHE · ABSAROKEE (CROW) · ARIKARA · OMAHA

1. Tense, tight and strained vocal style.
2. Northern Plains tribes prefer high vocal range while Southern Plains tribes prefer a medium range.
3. "Tumbling strain": melodies begin very high, drop drastically lower over the course of the song, presence of minor thirds; frequently end with repetitions of most important note.
4. Rapid changes in pitch and volume as well as pulsation of notes frequently occurs.
5. "Trills" are produced by rapidly fluttering the tongue against the roof of the mouth.
6. Singing is mostly unison.
7. Normally, one large drum is used to accompany music and is played by several people.
8. Flutes and whistles are used.
9. Bells on regalia create incidental musical sounds.

GREAT BASIN AND PLATEAU:

UTE · PAIUTE · WASHOE · GOSHUTE

1. Vocal style resembles Plains' style except in a lower range with a noticeable "growling" timbre and more relaxed throat.
2. Accompaniments are simple.
3. Melodious; include melodic rise.
4. Songs are short and repetitious.

NORTHWEST COAST:

TSIMSHIAN · TLINGIT · KWAKIUTL · HAIDA

1. Percussion rhythms are frequently quite complex.
2. Elaborately staged dramas feature song, dance, intricately carved masks with moving parts.
3. Drums include slit boxes and long hollowed logs.
4. Song forms and melodies are complex and may include chromatic intervals; some change key upwards as they progress.
5. Some polyphony occurs.

CALIFORNIA:

DIEGUENO · MOJAVE · YUROK · POMO

1. Vocal range is usually low with a relaxed singing style.
2. The singing is mostly solo with some occasional examples of polyphony found in the northern part of the region.
3. Rattles are used more frequently for accompaniment than are drums.

SOUTHWEST:

PUEBLO · ZUNI · HOPI · NAVAJO/APACHE · YAQUI

Description of Southwest music is usually divided into "Pueblo" and "Navajo/Apache" due to the differences in these styles which coexist in the same geographic region.)

PUEBLO:

1. Vocal style is similar to Plains, with a lower range and a more "growling" timbre.
2. Melodies are lengthy; tempo may change during song.
3. Vocal tension and pulsation are frequent throughout songs.
4. Varying sized drums are used, usually played solo.
5. Most singing is unison.
6. Agricultural themes are common. Most rituals are directed toward crop cycles.

NAVAJO/APACHE:

1. Light nasal singing style is normal. A high falsetto is used by men singing roles of women in Yeibichai ceremonies.
2. Vocal ranges are mixed.
3. Frequent use of tones/intervals based on the natural overtone series.
4. Mostly unison singing with some responsorial singing.
5. Flutes and whistles are occasionally used.
6. Drums, water drums, rattles, and "bells" used as accompaniment.
7. The one- or two-stringed Apache violin is the only stringed instrument among Native American traditional cultures.
8. Elaborate, multi-day (in some cases nine days long) healing ceremonials including Blessingway, Enemyway, and Nightway that incorporate singing, dancing, chanting, and sandpainting, guided by highly-trained "practitioners" with phenomenal memories.

INSTRUMENTS

Drums, rattles, and other percussion are the best known and most frequently used instruments used in Native American music. Flutes and whistles are the most common melodic instruments although these have not been used by all Native American tribes. The Apache violin continues to be unique.

STRINGS

Tsii'edo'a'tl, "The Wood that Sings"–An Apache violin by Chesley Goseyun Wilson

DRUMS

Taos Drum

The Apache violin (frequently referred to as a "fiddle") is a bowed instrument made from the century plant stalk and one or two horsehair strings. Chesley Wilson, a San Carlos Apache who is the great-great-grandson of Cochise, is a master crafter and player of Apache flutes and violins who says he patterns his violins after those made by famous artisans of the past, including Geronimo. In 1992, the State of Arizona declared him a "Living Treasure" for his dedication to traditional Apache arts including silversmithing, woodworking, storytelling and music.

Present-day Yaqui musicians have adopted a mariachi-like ensemble that includes uniquely designed handcrafted violins as well as Mexican guitar-like instruments including the vihuela (vee-wéy-lah)—a ukelele- or small guitar-size body with five strings and a swollen v-shaped back—and the guitarron (gee-tah-rón), a large version of the vihuela with a bass range. (Both the vihuela and guitarron originated in Jalisco, Mexico and are used extensively in mariachi ensembles.)

Drums are the best-known type of Native American instrument. They are made in many sizes and shapes as well as of diverse materials (pottery, logs, baskets, animal skins, etc.). The drum is considered by many Native Americans to represent the heartbeat of Mother Earth and it is also used to communicate with the supernatural. The Yaqui link the beat of the drum to the heartbeat of the deer, the animal essential to many of their ceremonies, dances and lore.

A typical drum is that used by the Pueblo peoples of the Southwest. Traditionally these have been made from sections of cottonwood logs and rawhide. First, an appropriate length and width of log is cut and hollowed out. Skin heads are placed on each end of the drum and laced together with leather lacing. The wood body of the drum may be decorated or painted with traditional designs or left plain. The beater consists of wool or cotton covered by leather and attached to a stick (usually also from the cottonwood tree).

26

The larger drums found among Plains tribes often have only the top covered with skin and the bottom left open for more resonance. They might be as large as a coffee-table, slung on a special stand or rack. Frequently, several people play this type of drum simultaneously with long beaters covered at the head with padded hide. In present-day pow-wow performances, the term "Drum" usually refers to not only the instrument itself, but to the performers who play it and sing. The "Drum" would then be the instrument, players, and singers. Many pow-wows feature a host Drum, who welcome groups to the gathering, and alternate playing and singing with them.

HAND DRUMS

Tarahumara Drum

Hand drums are common among many tribes. The style of stringing hand drums of the eastern tribes may allow pitch changes similar to those of the African hour-glass shaped talking drum. Drummers compete in drum challenges to determine the most creative performances on the instrument. Hand drums and frame drums found along the Northwest Coast and into Alaska may be square or round, often with elaborately criss-crossed thonging in back that both stretches and secures the skin and also creates a knotted handle. Some hand drums have a wooden handle protruding from the rim, others are held at the rim itself. Some of the skins have vestiges of fur remaining, some are scraped clean and left plain, others are painted with designs or symbols.

WATER DRUMS

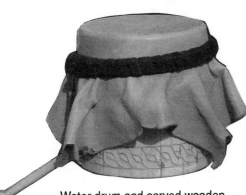

Water drum and carved wooden beater from the Six Nations Reserve, Ontario, Canada.

Water drums are found among many tribes, and are quite unusual in sound and appearance. The groups living in the Eastern Woodlands, the Iroquois (including the Seneca, Cayuga, Onondaga, Mohawk and Tuscarora) and Ojibway (Chippewa) among them, hollow out logs of varying width and height. On occassion, a small cask or keg might be used. Size varies from a small palm-held drum with a pinging sound, to large drums—as large as two feet high and eighteen inches in diameter—with a deep-sounding bass note. The bark often remains intact. Most have a plug for letting the water out. A varying amount of water is placed in the drum to affect both resonance and pitch. The drumhead is a soft length of bucksin or chamois, dipped in the water and stretched over the top of the drum. This skin is held on with a thong or hoop pushed tightly down over it. The voice of the drum is affected by how wet the skin is as well as how tightly it is pulled, and by the amount and temperature of the water. Sometimes coals are placed in the instrument to heat the water.

Among the Navajo and Apache, water drums are more commonly made of clay or iron pots, respectively. Navajo tradition requires that a piece of turquoise and another medicine stone be placed in each clay water drum, which in some cases has previously been used for cooking. The Apache iron pot drum is much larger than the Navajo, with a bigger voice, and is commonly played by more than one person. Some of these metal pot drums are typically used in the peyote religious ceremonies.

Water drum beaters include looped and twisted flexible branches; narrow, carved sticks; curved sticks, curved sticks which incorporate rattles, and more standard beaters.

27

NATIVE AMERICAN DRUMS AND RATTLES

Tuscarora octagonal-shaped drum.

Micmac single head hand drum. The beater is attached to the drum with a length of rawhide. The head is tacked on.

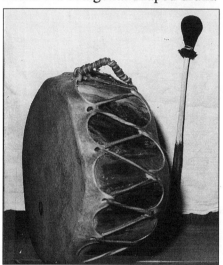

Cochiti Drum. The two heads are stretched tightly by the rawhide thong stringing. This type of drum has a very rich sound.

(Top) Ute Rawhide rattle; (L to R): Cherokee tortoise shell rattle, Iroquois horn rattle, Tigua gourd rattle, contemporary decorated gourd rattles.

RATTLES AND OTHER PERCUSSION

Hopi Owl Kachina Rattle

Rattles are the most ubiquitous type of instrument among Native Americans and display great inventiveness with natural materials. Whether made of gourds, turtle shells, carved wood, animal horns, deer hooves (sometimes suspended from deer antlers that have been shed), metal containers, rattlesnake rattles, bird beaks, animal bones, sea shells, spider casings, bent or molded hides or tree bark, modern Native Americans have incorporated virtually every type of material imaginable! (Turtle shell rattles are very interesting in that the number of segments on the top shell represents the number of moons—thirteen— in the lunar year. Some turtle shell rattles have seven segments on the stomach, which is the number of clans in many tribes.)

Almost anything that can make a percussive sound has been incorporated into the range of possibilities for musical accompaniment. Bells, scrapers, rasps, jaw bones, split-stick clappers, and bull-roarers (pieces of wood whirled rapidly through the air on a string to create a haunting hum) have been found among various tribes. Strings of sea shells, coins, bits of metal, and rocks are used either as a separate instrument to be shaken or as part of a dance costume.

The Apaches of Arizona fix sleigh-bells and shaped pieces of metal onto various parts of their dance costumes to add rattling effects. Years ago, jingles were cut from the tobacco tins and tin cans obtained from traders. Now the local grocery or mail-order craft-supply house provides a convenient source of "genuine Copenhagen snuff can lids" as the preferred jingle material. Cut and left flat, or rolled, then attached to strips of leather which are incorporated in distinctive patterns on the dance costume, jingles have a unique sound.

Rasps are used by many groups, and range from a notched stick or dowel, (which might be long and skinny or the diameter of a small baseball bat) to a grooved dried gourd. Yaqui musicians perform on a notched piece of wood, scraped with another stick, with an inverted gourd or bowl used as a resonator. The gourd or bowl might, in turn, be set in a container of water to enhance the sound. Legend states that the first Yaqui found two deer fighting in the woods. The sound of the antlers scraping became the rasp. The sound of the hooves kicking became the rattle. The sound of the heart beating became the drum. Some Plains tribes use a larger rasp placed against the drum head to produce a sound resembling the growling of a bear for use in the Bear Dance.

NATIVE AMERICAN FLUTES

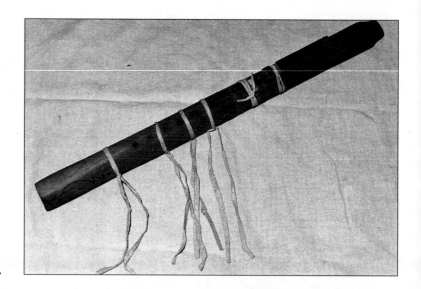

Kiowa flute.

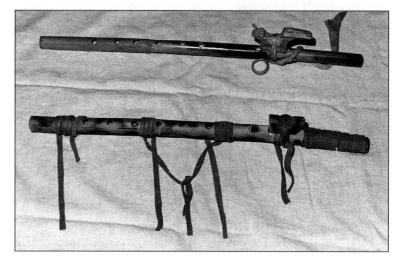

Top: Yavapai Apache Flute
Bottom: Cheyenne Flute

Top: Flute by Philip Carter
showing detail of "bird" carved
in the shape of a bird
Bottom: the entire flute.

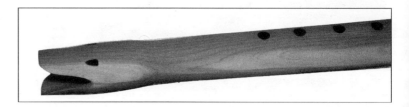

Detail of the loon head on a flute
made by Bear MacFarlane

FLUTES

Flutes are not used by all Native Americans. Plains and Southwest tribes have been most closely identified as employing flutes and whistles, particularly the Lakota, Kiowa and Comanche. There is also a significant flute tradition among the Ojibway (Chippewa). Most often, the instruments are made of wood or cane, however, some old clay and metal instruments exist. Flutes originated among the Plains tribes as courtship instruments although the instrument is now used for all types of music. Among the Kiowa, an ancient tradition of healing exists that incorporates flute songs. Animal bone whistles (frequently bird bones) have been used in dances.

Plains tradition traces the origin of the flute to an orphan boy. The child had few friends and spent much time alone in the woods. He was told by the Creator to carve a flute from a tree branch and to take his music from nature so he would always have a good tune. Many flute songs are imitations of bird calls and other natural sounds. Commercial recordings of Native American music frequently include sounds such as rain, thunder, birds, insets, etc. continuing to take music from nature.

Throughout the Southwest, pictographs of a flute player, Kokopelli, are found on canyon walls and rock formations. This mythical being was important in rituals guaranteeing rain and fertility. Kokopelli played his flute to restore balance in the universe and thereby insure rain and fertility.

The design of each Native American flute is highly individual. In general, however, there are three to six finger holes placed to produce pitches desired by the player. Each player generally attempts to match the instrument to his voice and songs. No uniform scalar system exists for the traditional flute although some modern commercial flutes are built on a western diatonic scale. The Native American flute is end-blown like the European recorder with pitches produced by covering and uncovering tone holes. Instruments are frequently elaborately decorated by the individual with designs including birds, animals, and mystical symbols. You will find a more complete discussion of the flute tradition including types, legends, flute makers and players as well as five flute songs in the chapter "Songs of the Wind: The Native American Flute."

LIVING WITH TRADITION

Top left:
Ruby Olson,
leader of the
Haliwa-Saponi
Dancers,
wearing a dress with
contemporary-style
dance jingles.

Top right:
Acoma Intercultural
Dancers drummers
(L-R): Tyrone
Gaisthea,
Bellamino Vicente,
Orin Dewahe.

Bottom left:
Berni Keyyope,
leader of the Acoma
Intercultural Dancers,
performing a Social
Dance.

Bottom right:
Alden Keyope of the
Acoma Intercultural
Dancers, performing
a Buffalo Dance,
holding a gourd
rattle, and wearing
tied-on dance bells.

Photo on the previous page: The Drum at a Cherokee pow-
wow. Sons learn the intricacies of the rhythms and songs
on the laps and by the sides of fathers, uncles and friends.
(Photo: John Running © 1991)

THE INTER-TRIBAL POW-WOW
UNITING THE CIRCLES

THE POW-WOW

A Celebration of Native American Culture

The term "pow-wow" in its use to describe a large gathering of Native Americans apparently originated in New England during the Seventeenth Century. Early colonists, including Roger Williams, observed gatherings around Narraganset (an east coast tribe residing in what is now Rhode Island) medicine men as they practiced their skills and the word "pawwaw" was overheard frequently. The colonists mistakenly took the meaning of the expression as reference to the meeting rather than the man who caused it. Through this popular usage, "pow-wow" became accepted by Native Americans as the English translation referring to their various celebrations.

Modern pow-wows are celebrations of Native American culture and include displays of tribal arts and crafts, serving meals of traditional Native foods, discussions of Native issues, and song, dance, and drum events. The basic theme of today's pow-wow is one of friendship and unity among all tribes.

Music and dance styles of the modern pow-wow are derived from those of the Plains tribes. Because of the strong efforts by the U.S. Government to eradicate Native American culture, many elements of dance, music, and religion, as well as life-style were lost to many tribes—particularly those east of the Mississippi. (The Bureau of Indian Affairs, from the 1880s until 1934 sought to ban all performances of Native music and religious celebrations. Many ceremonies literally died with their last practitioners.)

With the advent of "Wild West Shows" (the most famous of which was Buffalo Bill's Wild West Show) in the late nineteenth century, eastern tribes began to learn songs and dances from "Real Live Indians" travelling as part of the entertainment troupes. As most of these performers were from the northern Plains tribes, the songs and dances they passed on were from their culture.

It was at this time, also, that east coast tribes began to

adopt some of the characteristic dress, including the eagle feather bonnet, of the Plains.

Following the lifting of bans on Native culture in 1934 some elements of traditional styles began to re-emerge among all tribes. Performers sought research data regarding their customs and attempted to reconstruct rituals and music based on earlier descriptions. Unfortunately, complete rituals were not always available and, in some cases, no living tribal members had participated in such events and, in several cases, no tribal members could speak the original tribal language to interpret meanings of materials which could be found.

The number and kinds of dances performed at a pow-wow vary considerably. Northern and Southern style pow-wows have slightly different formats and dances. Some of the types of dances frequently performed include the following:

GRAND ENTRY: Usually a "slow war dance" during which all dancers and singers enter the arena.

FLAG SONG: Honoring song similar in concept to a national anthem

MEN'S TRADITIONAL DANCE: Dancers perform in regalia which is a replica of "old" dress (often pre-reservation). The dances are individually conceived and may represent war exploit, hunting exploit, or simply express pride in heritage.

WOMEN'S TRADITIONAL DANCE: Dancers perform in buckskin dresses (although some cloth dresses may be seen). Dance movements are graceful and show pride in heritage. Small up and down movements of the shoulders are common, as is an upright stance. Northern style traditional dancers often remain stationary with slight movements while Southern style traditional dancers move around the dance arena. The women may carry a folded shawl over one bent forearm, or hold a small bundle of objects with special significance to them while they dance. The dancers appear to be deeply absorbed in the experience.

MEN'S FANCY WAR DANCE: Dancers' regalia is elaborate and features prominent bustles, fancy beadwork, and striking color combinations. The dance style is exciting and limited only by the imagination of the dancer.

FANCY SHAWL DANCE: This is the women's version of fancy dancing. Beautifully designed shawls with embroidery, woven designs or beadwork, feature prominently in the dancers' regalia and the dance steps display high steps, intricate turns, and much individual creativity. As the women dance, they move the shawls gracefully, or hold them in such a way that the fringes around the edges bounce in lively harmony with the steps.

GRASS DANCE: Dance regalia is distinguished by porcupine-hair ribbons, yarn, fancy beadwork, feathers and sometimes little mirrors that flash as the dancers move. Large sleigh-bells typically are tied onto the dancers' legs with a leather strap. Many grass dancers carry a special bundle or stick in one hand, and move it in stylized patterns. Originally, the energetic grass dancers were the first in the dance arena (which might be a field or meadow, or a former arena that had not been used recently and was covered with long grass) and flattened the grass down with their stamping footsteps before the rest of the dancers entered. The ribbons and yarn decoration represent scalps which were originally part of the regalia when war veterans were accorded the honor of entering the arena first. In competition, the grass dancers must try to end their steps firmly on the final drumbeat.

JINGLE DANCE: The steps to this dance resemble those of the Fancy Shawl Dance. The regalia features many "jingles" made from metal disks (often the lids of snuff cans, soup cans, etc.) suspended from the outfit by rawhide or yarn strands.

HOOP DANCE: The Hoop Dance is an individual dance. The performer uses from five to sixty hoops to deftly create intricate patterns representing animals and plants which give aid to human beings. The dance is said to represent the emergence of humans into this world. Manipulating the hoops while simultaneously dancing requires tremendous dexterity. Many hoop dancers interweave all of their hoops at the end of a sequence of figures to create a representation of the globe with the interlocking circles of all living things. Well-respected hoop dancers include Kevin Locke, Marty Goodbear, and Eddie Swimmer (of the American Indian Dance Theater).

EAGLE DANCE: This dance honors the eagle. Dancers' regalia includes wings made of eagle feathers and a mask designed to look like an eagle head. Movements imitate flying, soaring, and hopping of the eagle.

INTER-TRIBAL SOCIAL DANCES: There are a variety of social dances including Round Dances, Rabbit Dances, and "Forty-Niner" songs (see "Introduction to Round

Dances" for a closer look at Forty-Niner songs). The social dances are the ones that are least likely to have restrictions in terms of who may participate. In some cases, the focus of the dance is the appreciation of the interconnectedness of life—the acknowledgment of the dance circle as a reflection of the ties within the community. The Two-Step resembles the square dance format with elements of Native American dances incorporated. There are line dances much like the Virginia Reel, particularly dances in the Southwest and Plains, although the Eastern Woodlands groups rarely dance in lines. The round (or circle) dances move generally counterclockwise in the Eastern Woodlands and the Southwest. However, in the Plains and northern California, round dances typically proceed clockwise.

*Note: *We have used the word "regalia" instead of "costume" because, as one dancer put it, "Regalia is what we dance in; costumes are what we wear for Halloween."*

ATTENDING A POW WOW

Attending a Native American pow-wow or cultural fair is one of the most effective means of gaining a greater understanding of this vibrant culture. Admission charges are usually quite low and visitors are encouraged to attend.

Museums, tribal councils, and cultural centers are frequently sponsors of Native American performances and gatherings. If a reservation or significant population of Native Americans exists near your location, calendars of events will be available from the tribal government or Native American Center. These events might also be listed in the entertainment section of the newspaper.

National listings of pow-wows are most easily found in such Native American periodicals as *Whispering Wind* (8009 Wales Street, New Orleans, Louisiana 70126) and *News from Indian Country* (Rt. 2 Box 2900-A, Hayward, Wisconsin 54843). *Native American Cooperative* (PO Box 5000Z, San Carlos AZ 85550-0301) has very complete listings. *Akwesasne Notes*, (Mohawk Nation, via Rooseveltown, NY 13683) includes a calendar, articles, a mail-order service and environmental news. These national publications also contain informative articles covering Native American political and social concerns as well as cultural information.

After selecting an event to attend, keep in mind a few simple procedures to avoid potential embarrassment and to make attendance more meaningful:

1. Dress appropriately. Most Native Americans stress modesty and encourage conservative dress. For example, the Navajoland Tourism Office suggests that shorts, halter tops, bathing suits, etc. not be worn while attending events or while visiting the reservation.

2. Refrain from taking photographs or making recordings unless permission is granted. Most pow-wows allow reasonable photography at public events, but specific restrictions may exist. Photographs usually may not be taken during a "flag song," "Veterans' honoring song," or a "pick up" dance. Public announcements are generally made requesting that photography not take place at these times or during other specified times. If an individual seems to be avoiding your camera, respect the individual's wishes. When in doubt, ask permission of the individual or group.

3. Observe any restrictions on seating or viewing areas. Often, the first few rows of seats around the dance arena are reserved for dancers and singers. Do not stand in front of these seats and block access to the arena.

4. Do not attempt to join in the dancing unless you are specifically invited by one of the participants or there is a general announcement inviting public participation. Several times during a pow-wow, visitors will be invited to learn dances or take part in activities—the Native Americans are proud of their culture and wish to spread knowledge and understanding. However, many, if not most, dances at the event will be either competitive or serve a ceremonial purpose.

5. Browse through the crafts booths. Show respect for the cultural items displayed for sale and avoid any insensitive comments concerning materials or designs. Recently, some non-Indian visitors have criticized craftsmen for use of animal fur and parts in apparel and crafts. Keep in mind that you are a guest in another culture!

6. Alcohol is prohibited at many pow-wows.

7. Ask questions. Most Native Americans are willing to share knowledge about their culture. Some information, however, is restricted to religious initiates or members of a specific tribe. If an individual is reluctant to discuss something, respect his/her beliefs and do not pursue the issue.

8. Above all: respect, observe and appreciate.

Right:
Although many dancers today have adopted the dress characteristic of the Plains nations, Anthony Dean Stanton (right) and his uncle, Richard Wilcox, have created regalia for themselves which reflects their Narragansett heritage. Anthony is wearing his wolf regalia which he described as "truly eastern." He carries the shell of a snapping turtle. Like the Narragansett who live on the coast and took their living from both ocean and river creatures "turtles live in both fresh and sea water. Our people have always had the story of the world being carried on the back of a great turtle."

In competition where "style counts" dancers wearing the more elaborate plains regalia often have an advantage. Wanting to compete, but still maintain his Narragansett identity, Richard has taken a basic eastern style and updated it through the use of dramatic color, using pure white buckskin and fox pelts.

Below:
Paul Roaring Winds performs "Sneak-up," a Lakota men's dance which has been adopted inter-tribally. He moves close to the ground, recreating the act of sneaking up "on an enemy or on food."

Photographs by Claudia Chapman

40

Photo on the previous page: Hundreds of people—men, women, and children—from a number of different nations join together to celebrate new and old traditions wearing regalia that has been painstakingly crafted, oftentimes by the wearer. Scene: the Little Shell Pow-wow, Fort Berthold, North Dakota.
(Photo: John Running © 1986)

MOVING IN THE CIRCLE
SONGS AND DANCES

PRIVACY AND USAGE

A note about the Contributors

All of the songs and dances in this collection are in current usage and were learned in the traditional Native American manner. Many of them would not be called "traditional" in the sense of "ancient." Rather, these are contemporary, being sung now in many versions in many places and with many divergent opinions of their origins. They are the songs the people are singing at informal gatherings, in the back of a pick-up truck, in the shade of a tree, at a school or cultural center demonstration, and of course, at modern pow-wows. In each case, a specific individual, performer or group taught the material by demonstration, actively involving the learner—a "learn by doing" approach. These guides were eminently patient and nurtured "students" encouragingly through each step from first efforts to mastery. That each song be learned accurately seemed more important—regardless of time involved—than simple expediency. I have chosen to include primarily social songs—none are religious, although a few (such as the first, "Song to the Four Directions") have something more than a purely social function. As you will see in the descriptive notes for individual dances those that might have possible ceremonial use were moved out of context or altered in some way by the singers to make them appropriate for inclusion in these pages. The origins cited for each song are those given by the original source, people who are actively using, and hearing others use, the songs. It is, of course, possible that some errors may unwittingly have been made. The singer/teacher may have learned the song from another person who learned it from yet another singer and so forth until the origins of the song have become obscured. In addition, the function of a particular song may have changed at some point in the transmission process. This is but one of the difficulties encountered when conducting research in an oral culture. All of the singers who shared these songs with me were aware that all materials learned would be used in educational settings ranging from classrooms to clinics and publications. Each agreed with the importance of teaching about their culture and values and were eager to participate in the dissemination of such knowledge. They hope you will approach each selection with the same respectful attitude in which it was offered. The debt owed to these individuals is beyond expression.

There are, however, other members of the Native American culture who are hesitant to reveal any cultural information and who strongly object to use of any materials by non-Indians, or out-of-context use. These same individuals might criticize (and sometimes even ostracize) other Native Americans who choose to assist in projects such as this collection and might challenge the veracity of the information and the appropriateness with which it is used. To protect my sources from such criticism, or for those who desire to maintain their privacy even as they are committed to sharing their repertoire, many are not identified by name; occasionally, a composite source has been created for the purposes of discussion of the material. Researchers who commonly work with Native American matters understand and frequently take these, or similar, precautions, including the use of code numbers, assigned names, or descriptions such as "Lakota woman, age 27."

LYRICS

About the texts to the songs in this resource

Most of the songs in this collection use only vocables as lyrics. Among the reasons for this approach are that that this is the original format of the song as I learned it, or that the source providing the song wished to substitute vocables for texts because of personal spiritual beliefs or other deeply held considerations. In the latter cases, vocables which resemble the original text phonetically have been used. In the case of "I Walk in Beauty" and "One-Eyed Ford," the English lyrics are those provided by the singers. The translations for other songs are also provided by the original sources.

Some users of this resource might be disappointed that singable English lyrics have not been created and may regard the songs with only or primarily vocables as intrinsically inferior or as having inconsequential meaning. Nothing is farther from the truth.

The lack of lyrics in the Western sense should not be interpreted to mean the song's vocables are silly, *non*-sense syllables and that such songs are thus to be taken lightly. The vocables may be remnants of an older language, part of ritual formulae, or represent unworded communication on a more spiritual plane. Sometimes, single words or phrases may be interpolated into the stream of vocable sounds. The

44

introduction of the single word "rain," for example, may not have great meaning to the casual listener. This single word, however, conveys much cultural and spiritual information to the Native American: prayer for rain; giving thanks for rain; using the word as symbolic for "life-bringing." A literal translation may include but a few words while the understood meaning of the word or phrase may be so complex as to require a virtual thesis for explanation. This type of cultural shorthand is found in music of many cultures, notably throughout Africa. Language and thought structure in most Native American languages is not readily understood in terms of the Western Indo-European family of languages. To a Native American perhaps only one or two well-chosen words are required to express a sophisticated, complex concept because of the implied shared understanding of cultural significance among initiated listeners.

There are many Native American songs which have lyrics primarily or entirely in the language of the singer. I chose not to include them until I develop greater fluency in these languages. Some phrases and words are included in the Appendix. If you are interested in learning more about the many Native American languages, contact the American Indian College Fund, cultural centers or museums in your area for information about formal and informal classes. Canyon Records and Indian Arts in Phoenix, Arizona, markets two language tape sets: *Beginning Cherokee* and *Conversational Lakota*. A book/tape set *Conversational Navajo* is available from the Navajo Tribal Museum bookstore in Window Rock, Arizona. Addresses for these and other sources are listed in the Appendix.

⋀⋁⋀⋁⋀⋁⋀⋁⋀⋁⋀⋁⋀
NOTATION
AND
PRONUNCIATION

Notation for these songs, of necessity, is approximate. As this is music from an aural tradition, singing techniques are not limited to those easily represented by standard Western notation. There are portamenti, bends, drops, swoops, catches, etc. occurring throughout the songs. Use the companion tapes to identify and absorb these techniques.

For most of the songs, vocables have been used as text. In some cases, vocables have been substituted for text at the request of the informant. The following pronunciation guide should help you sing through the written version of each song, however, you should listen carefully to the tape to hear and learn the rhythmic nuances and subtleties of pronunciation, particularly those sounds not commonly encountered in the English language.

VOWELS:

"e" as in b*e*t; "a" as in f*a*ther; "i" as in sk*i*; "o" as in d*o*n't; "u" as in fl*u*te

The **"h"** preceding some vocables is more a preparatory rush of air than an articulated consonant. "Hwe" would not be exactly "whey" as in "curds and whey" but more "huh—way" with a rush of air for "h" blending into the first note on "we." The tape will help you hear this more clearly. This might be compared to the air sound many music teachers hear beginning instrumentalists make when started a pitch—there is the sound of air, then the note begins.

The **"yo"** in several songs should not be pronounced *a la* Sly Stallone! The "y" is usually the natural result of pitch changes and the reformation of the mouth and tongue necessary to pronounce the "o." For example, "he-yo" would not be two clearly articulated sounds (hey, yoh) as the "y" is merely a transitional sound occuring between the "e" and the "o." Again, the tape will clarify this.

VARIANTS

A reality of the Oral/Aural tradition

If there is any maxim which applies to the performance of Native American social songs and dances, it surely must be: "Nothing is carved in stone." Versions of any given Native American song will vary from performer to performer and even from performance to performance by the same person. The changes may be a subtle as adjusting the range or rhythms for a specific voice, but may include far more involved structural variation.

Although differences in tribal and regional style account for many variations, perhaps the majority of differences in these social songs and dances result from the oral transmission of the music from performer to performer. Native American music is not usually learned from notation, but from repetition of the song in a rote learning process. Songs and dances are passed from generation to generation. Originally, a parent uncle or aunt filled this role, but in modern times, native American schools and cultural centers are taking the lead in the preservation of traditional arts. A singer familiar with the song will pass it to a new singer, repeating it as necessary. Elders teach young folks. Individuals learn by observation during a ceremonial event. As the song passes from singer to singer, the melody might evolve adjusting to each singer's style or preference.

As the song moves from tribe to tribe, further variations may occur including changes in accompaniment, substitution of vocables for text, substitution of text for vocables, or changes in vocables. The singing style and even content may change as the song moves through the Native American community, reflecting changing current events or specific personal, social or ceremonial needs.

46

All of these factors, of course, are to be found in folk and popular musics throughout the world. A simple example in western popular music is that both Frank Sinatra and Elvis Presley recorded "My Way,"but there are significant differences in their respective performances. (After listening to Sinatra and Presley, listen to a marching band arrangement of "My Way.")

The same types of variants discovered in songs are also found in dances of Native Americans for many of the same reasons. Regional stylistic preferences, tastes or skills of performers have a significant effect. A major cultural factor explaining the acceptance of such great diversity in style and skill level of the performer is that the Native American culture sets no one standard for individual perfection. Individual differences are respected and no "fault" assigned to those who may be less flamboyant in performance than others. In cases where the dance (or song) is ceremonial and requires highly accurate performance, each individual is assigned a role in the "performance" suited to his/her gifts so that all may participate and all will be successful.

Social dances are frequently quite creative—a Two-Step may evolve to a Round Dance and back or the shape of a Round Dance may change to a spiral or zig-zag to accommodate the number of participants. The ingenuity of the lead couple may also lead to innovative changes in the dance steps.

These materials were learned in the traditional way in a variety of settings ranging from the back of a pick-up truck bouncing through Monument Valley to formal public performances—yes, the Native Americans will invite one to participate and learn several dances at each performance. One troupe leader advises good naturedly that he always seeks volunteers from those audience members moving toward the back of the room or trying to hide behind friends. The joking rejoinder that anyone refusing to dance has to pay five dollars to the person who invites participation goes back to the traditional practice of giving a gift (usually money) to your female partner before being allowed to stop dancing. (See "When Attending a Pow-Wow" in Chapter 3. If you attend a dance session, pow-wow, or ceremonial event, be sensitive to whether the general audience is being welcomed as participants, or whether specific cultural or organizational affiliation is required for any particular song/dance.)

SONG TO THE FOUR DIRECTIONS

He   ya he ya ya he ya he ya he yo - he ya he. ya

he ya he ya he yo - he yahe. ya he ya he ya he yo - he ya he.

Slower

ya ho -   ya he -   ya ho -   ya he.

SONG TO THE FOUR DIRECTIONS

OBSERVED: East Texas, early 1980s

GROUP: Alabama-Coushatta

RECORDING: "Song to the Four Directions" on the companion tape.

BACKGROUND:

The Alabama-Coushatta presently live on a 4,700 acre reservation some ninety miles northeast of Houston. The Alabamas and Coushattas are closely related Muskogean tribes originating in the southeast woodlands of Mississippi and Alabama with western contact documented as early as the explorations of Hernando de Soto in 1541.

During the late eighteenth and early nineteenth centuries, the tribes migrated to their present homeland in the Big Thicket region of east Texas. The reservation was established in 1855. After they arrived in Texas, the Alabama-Coushatta became known as "Sam Houston's Indians"—a source of tribal pride to the present day. To live on the reservation and receive full benefits, tribal members must be full-blooded Indian, making this one of the strictest groups in terms of establishing membership. The united tribes operate a strong tourist center featuring dances, visits to craft shops, and tours of the Big Thicket Swamp. Although the dances performed at the tourist facility are primarily derived from Plains and Pueblo styles, several members of the tribe actively seek to preserve their original music. In the early 1980s I taught at a high school in East Texas near the Alabama-Coushatta Reservation and became well-acquainted with tribal members. Several shared information concerning the tribes and the culture, including this song.

In most performances or ceremonies, participants will dedicate the area in which the dancing and singing will take place before any performances begin, usually starting with the acknowledgement of the four directions. This song does not accompany a dance, *per se*, but is a typical way to create the appropriately respectful attitude that is considered the foundation for a gathering or event.

DANCE INSTRUCTIONS:

This song to the Four Directions is a musical offering honoring the four directions: East—in which the sun rises; South—from which the light comes; West—where the sun sets; and North—from which the cold comes. (Tribes also associate specific times of life, colors, types of power or healing as coming from each direction; however each tribe does not necessarily duplicate the interpretation of the others.) The song is sung very freely with the dotted-eighth/sixteenth rhythm being quite ambivalent (as in jazz) and a gliding "portamento" between notes on the syllable "yo." During the last section of the song, the singer faces each direction with the right hand lifted, palm upwards, as if in supplication. The direction is changed during the rest following each fermata.

I WALK IN BEAUTY

I WALK IN BEAUTY

OBSERVED: Flagstaff, Arizona, gathering; 1989

GROUP: Apache/Navajo

MUSIC: "I Walk in Beauty" on the companion tape; composed by Arlene Nofchissey Williams

BACKGROUND:

Navajo believe humanity to be part of a delicately balanced universe in which all forms of life as well as natural elements interrelate and interact with no part being either more or less important than another. The Navajo refer to this concept as *hozho*, (technically spelled Hózhóó or Hózhóón) which is commonly translated as "beauty" although the concept has little to do with popular ideas of what beauty means. It does not refer to physical attractiveness, fashion sense or hair style. It is an inner state of being, that can manifest itself in a life and attitudes. (Many world traditions recognize this state with a special word.) When an individual maintains this balance, one is said to "walk in Beauty."

When the balance is upset—only humans can upset the balance—a special rite is performed for the general well-being of an individual or group. Upon completion of these extremely complex rites, the individual again "walks in Beauty" or is in balance (harmony) with the universe.

This song was written by Arlene Nofchissey Williams, Navajo, and was first recorded several years ago on a commercial recording of the Lamanite Generation produced at Brigham Young University, which many Native American students attend. It is now commonly sung at pow-wows in many languages and versions, invested with feelings of genuine good will. It is not part of any traditional Navajo ceremony, but incorporates phrases based on poetry used in a rite. The English lyrics used in this song do not accurately reflect the deeply religious concept of hozho held by many traditional Navajo. These words, however, should be considered neither as portraying actual religious belief nor as a trivialization of such beliefs. This is simply a song with great currency in the southwestern United States. The concept of seeking universal harmony is expressed in the text which is related to the following (poetic) translation of a fragment of the actual lengthy chant:

> *In Beauty I walk*
> *With Beauty before me, I walk*
> *With Beauty behind me, I walk*
> *With Beauty above me, I walk*
> *With Beauty all around me, I walk*
> *With Beauty within me, I walk*
> *In Beauty, it is finished.*

Those from the Western cultures too often have sought to restructure "primitive" cultures according to Western models, failing to recognize the depth and beauty of the Native philosophies and beliefs. All humankind can well heed the call for universal harmony present in Native American culture, put aside the centuries-long reluctance to learn from this culture, and seek to "walk in Beauty."

This version of "I Walk in Beauty" was learned from an Apache woman singer performing during a gathering in Flagstaff, Arizona. The song was sung in honor of the Navajo with verses in Apache, Navajo, and English. Members of the "audience" rose in honor of all people and some began a simple movement resembling the Friendship Dance described below. Even those unfamiliar with the words, hummed or "sang" along, each making an individual contribution to the joining of all peoples in universal harmony and peace.

FRIENDSHIP DANCE

OBSERVED: Flagstaff Pow-Wow • Arizona; July, 1990.

GROUP: Western Apache

RECORDING: "I Walk in Beauty" as performed by Western Apache singers on the companion tape. A transcription of this song is included on the previous page. Almost any social or round dance song is appropriate for this dance, particularly those of the Navajo and Apache. In addition to songs of these types found in this collection, songs from numerous recordings listed in the discography may be used, including those on *Music of the White Mountain Apache* (Canyon).

BACKGROUND:

Although the group I observed performing this dance in Flagstaff were Apache, the dance itself is quite common among most western and Plains tribes. Dances designated as "friendship" dances have been documented from the mid-nineteenth century forward. The movement in each of these dances varies from the steps given below to a round dance version to more complicated couple dances. However, the theme of unity and friendship is common. This dance was learned at the Flagstaff Pow-Wow when I was selected to perform with the troupe by friends who had worked with me the previous summer—these Apache were the same who had given medical aid to the rather clumsy researcher (me) who had the misfortune to step on a sleeping rattlesnake. The observers had a thoroughly good time enjoying a newly discovered version of the snake dance before giving help (the snake's fangs had become caught in the shoe leather and the victim was vigorously trying to shake the snake loose!!)

DANCE INSTRUCTIONS:

This dance allows great individual freedom for the participants by using the simplest version of the Friendship Dance:

   • A person may dance as an individual, as part of a couple, or as part of a larger group. The groups may be mixed gender or single gender. Groups are frequently couples, families, or simply groups of friends.
   • Members of the group may join hands, link arms, or let the arms hang freely by the sides.
   • Dancers or dance groups may—or may not—move forward and back at the same time.
   • The exact number of steps forward and back may vary with each dancer or group of dancers.
   Because of this flexibility, the Apache Friendship Dance may be effectively used to introduce group movement to young students, including those reluctant to participate in a "dance" situation. The purpose of the dance, to the Native American, is to express friendship with a special group of people, all dancers, or simply all humankind. Individual differences are deeply respected.
   May we all seek to walk in balance on the Earth and truly walk in the Pathway of Beauty.

BASIC MOVEMENT:

- Lines of dancers or groups of dancers face each other on opposite sides of the dance floor.
- Each dancer stands facing forward with knees slightly bent, back erect, and head held high.
- The movement is simply four to six steps forward and the same number back. The only "strict" requirement is the dancer move with the beat of the music. Each dancer participates at an individual level of skill and expression.

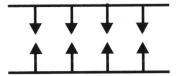 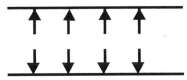

At Native American dances, this social dance can last for many hours!! Individuals and groups join and drop out of the dance periodically as the dance continues.

- Frequently, near the end of the dance (cued by special drum beats), all dancers have joined hands in a large circle. The dancers begin moving into a tighter circle, raising the arms as they move forward. Then, the group moves back gradually lowering the arms. The dance ends with a rush to the center with considerable "whooping" and merriment.

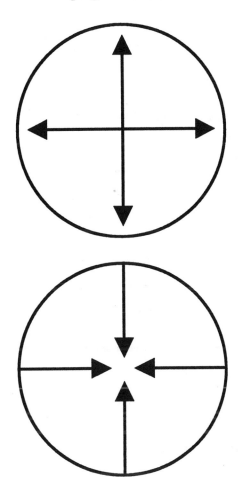

HALIWA-SAPONI CANOE DANCE

We ya we we ya we we ya we, Ya we ya o - we. Ya

we ya we we ya we we ya we, Ya we ya o - we. Ya we ha ya we ha

yo - we; Ya we ya o - we. Ya we ha ya we ha yo - we; Ya

we ya o - we. Ya we ya o - we.

HALIWA-SAPONI CANOE DANCE

OBSERVED: Bedford, Pennsylvania, September, 1989.

GROUP: Saponi; this version performed by the Haliwa-Saponi Singers, under the direction of Ruby Olsen (currently from York, PA) The group has existed for approximately fifteen years.

RECORDING: "Canoe Song" on companion tape.

BACKGROUND:

The Saponi originated in the mid-Atlantic region of the Eastern Woodlands. Small bands were found throughout the 1700s in North Carolina and Virginia. As pressure from encroaching white settlement grew, the Saponi migrated northward through Virginia, Maryland, and Pennsylvania, ultimately reaching New York where they were adopted by the Cayuga division of the Iroquois Confederation in 1753. The Haliwa-Saponi maintain a tribal office, day care center, and craft store in Hollister, North Carolina. "Haliwa" is derived from Halifax and Warren counties in North Carolina, the area where most of this group reside. A group of Haliwa-Saponi are frequent performers at pow-wows and Native American Cultural Fairs throughout the mid-east, often including relatives from Seneca and Tuscarora tribes (also part of the Iroquois group) as part of the ensemble. On one recent occasion, the group included one Navajo, one Sioux and one Seneca as well as several Saponi.

This performing group finances travel to friends and other vacation travel through these demonstrations and performances—often a blanket dance (a blanket is placed on the ground or carried through the crowd for contributions) is performed or an admission fee charged.

DANCE INSTRUCTIONS:

This dance imitates the motion of traveling in a canoe. The activity can be considered either as a game or instructional dance for children. (Native Americans have long used songs and dances to teach hunting and domestic skills.)

1. Several dancers form a single-file line behind a lead dancer. The second and subsequent dancers place hands on the waist of the preceding dancer. The hands may rest on the upper arms, if desired, rather than on the waist. (This dance group represents the paddlers in a canoe. Three or four dancers per group is a workable number.)

2. The groups move first to the left in a side-step motion:

```
L  R  L  R  L  R  L  R
1  +  2  +  3  +  4  +
```

Then to the right:

```
R  L  R  L  R  L  R  L
1  +  2  +  3  +  4  +
```

3. There is a forward motion led by the first dancer moving in a generally clockwise circle. The lead dancer serves as a "navigator" determining the path of the "canoe."

4. The elbows and arms move in a rowing motion, as if paddling the canoe.

5. Collisions might happen with a large group, but gradually, skillfully-maneuvered close calls will be the order of the day.

BEAR DANCE

OBSERVED: Many times. This version: Hollister, North Carolina, 1990

GROUP: Haliwa-Saponi

RECORDING: "Bear Dance" Haliwa-Saponi Singers, field recording. (Note the growls, screams and laughter!)

BACKGROUND:

Animal dances occur universally among the various Native American peoples. The purposes of these dances include insuring success in hunting the specific animal, seeking aid from the animal spirit (as in healing or causing rain), to honor the animal, and to thank the animal for help or allowing its body to be used for the benefit of the humans.

Audiences of the motion picture *Dances with Wolves* observed parts of a dance to seek success in hunting buffalo, and most who attend inter-tribal pow wows have seen versions of the Eagle Dance. Other familiar animal dances are the deer dances of the southwest and numerous versions of the Bear Dance.

The bear is revered by almost every Native American culture. Bears are often considered symbols of great power and strength and are frequently viewed as closely related to humans. Native Americans use bear grease as both a cosmetic and healing potion, the teeth and claws for ornaments, and the hide for clothing. Bear fetishes are prized among the Zuni and bear paw designs may be found on jewelry as well as in petroglyphs throughout the western United States.

Bears are an anomaly. They may be classified by Native Americans as both "two-legged" (human) and "four-legged" (animal). The physical similarities between an upright bear and a walking man are obvious as may be the similarity in diet including fish, game, and berries. The relationship of Human and Bear forms a part of the mythology of many tribes.

Bears are considered to be ancestors by the Utes who celebrate the emergence of bears from hibernation with an elaborate multi-day festival. Descriptions of both the ceremonial dances and social dances associated with this rite may be found in the book, *Indian Dances of North America* by Reginald and Gladys Laubin. The 1991 national tour by the American Indian Dance Theatre featured a performance of the Ute Bear Dance. A rasp is used to produce the sound of a growling bear as part of the accompaniment to this dance. The rasp is placed over a drum or basin to produce a more resonant sound and scraped with a second stick. Players are quite free to create as realistic a sound as possible while the dancer mimics the movements of a bear matching the intensity of the "growl." Often, to create the loudest possible sound, a pit is hollowed in the ground and a piece of sheet metal placed over it to create a large resonator for the bear rasp.

Southeastern Native Americans, such as the Cherokee, have a traditional belief that bears were once human and evolved into bears because of laziness and an unwillingness to accept the hardships and uncertainties of human existence. The following Cherokee tale explains how this came to happen:

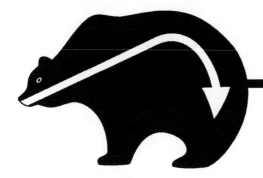

LEGEND
How Bears Came Into Being

Once there was a clan of humans who lived near the mountains of what the white people call the Carolinas. They lived through raising corn and hunting and endured all the pleasures and hardships of the traditional life. When crops and hunting were good, the humans lived well; when crops and hunting were bad, the humans suffered.

A small boy from one of the families began to spend more and more time away from the village, living in the mountains. When he returned home, he was was not hungry because "there is always plenty to eat in the mountains."

After a time, he spent days at a time in the mountains and began to grow hair all over his body because he was eating animal food rather than human food.

This development greatly disturbed his family and all members of the clan. When he was asked to explain why he preferred to live as an animal, he told his clan, "There is always plenty to eat in the mountains. There are always fish in the rivers, berries and roots in the woods, and fresh game. If we lived in the mountains, we wouldn't have to break our backs working to raise corn or have to spend weeks hunting meat. We wouldn't have to make and wear clothes because we would grow our own coats. If you want to live a life free of hard work and uncertainty, you will come and live with me in the mountains."

The clan members listened to his remarks and debated what to do. Finally, they decided to abandon their village and move to the hills. After fasting to purge their bodies of human food, they began to grow furry coats and roam, sometimes on two feet, sometimes on four. As they abandoned their human ways, they ate heavily and slept more often. Eventually they found that if they ate enough in summer, they could sleep through the entire winter when human suffering was at its greatest.

Members of related clans were puzzled over the disappearance of the village. When seeking their relations, they found hairy human-like beasts who still remembered some of their language. As a parting gift, the bears gave the tribe special songs and dances for hunting and honoring the bears.

Opposite:
Paul Roaring Winds, of Cree descent, wears a set of bear claws as part of his regalia. The bear holds particular significance for the Cree people whose homeland is the James Bay area of Canada.

BEAR DANCE

He e ha he ya, he e ha he ya.
[hey ey hah hey yah, hey ey hah hey yah

(Repeat song many times)

Ho whah cha no - o, ho wha cha no - o.
hoh whah chah noh oh hoh whah chah noh - oh]

Photo: Claudia Chapman

DANCE INSTRUCTIONS:

The Bear Dance described here is as performed by the Haliwa-Saponi of North Carolina. Characteristic of Southeastern Native American melodies, this song contains only four pitches and consists of numerous repetitions of short phrases. In performance, the song begins very softly and gradually increases in volume. After a high point is reached (after several repetitions), the volume diminishes with each subsequent repetition with a fade-out ending. Singers traditionally perform the first four measures in a chant-like style and use a more lyrical style for the final two measures.

The dancer, wearing a bear skin draped over his head and back, mimics movements of a bear including scrambling on four feet, rearing into the air, pawing the air, or eating berries from the ground or trees. Occasionally, the "bear" may "attack" an inattentive or disrespectful member of the audience. The more realistic the imitation of a bear by the dancer, the greater the honor to the bear spirit.

When the dancer is not imitating the gait of the bear, he uses a step-tap dance step familiar to all scouts who earned merit badges in "Indian dancing." The toe of the foot taps on the first half of the beat, raises slightly, then the foot is placed flat on the ground on the second half of each beat giving a:

L L R R
1 + 2 +   etc. sequence of steps.

A replica bear costume may be made for classroom use from the "faux fur" material available from fabric stores. The "fur" should be cut in the general shape of a bearskin and the edges stitched for reinforcement. The head of the bear may be fastened to a baseball cap (for ease in wearing) and eyes, nose, and mouth fashioned from appropriate craft materials. The size of the costume is not particularly important.

ROUND DANCES

INTRODUCTION:

Some type of round dance is universally found among modern Native American tribes. The circle has always had deep significance for Native Americans: moving clockwise in a circle is believed to be moving in harmony with the forces of creation; living "within the circle" refers to maintaining harmony with the universe and all nature; medicine wheels in a circular form are found throughout the continent; various circular designs are used to teach Native American ways.

Round dances have been given many names—Owl Dance, Round Dance, Circle Dance, Friendship Dance, Mother Earth Dance. The Owl Dance, for example, is a version performed by the Crow and related tribes in which the left foot is lifted on the accented beats rather than "stepped" as by other tribes thereby giving the impression of dancing "off the beat."

Several versions of the "Forty-Niner" are performed as a round dance, sometimes with joined hands or linked arms, at other times with hands placed on the shoulder of the next person. The name "Forty-Niner" is linked to many different explanations. It is said that it refers to a group of fifty Chippewa soldiers from Wisconsin who fought in World War I. Forty-nine returned from the war, and they and the memory of the one who did not return, were honored with special singing and dancing. Later, after the war, those who had served in the military returned with more dance styles learned from their non-Indian buddies. Forty-Niner songs are most common among the Plains peoples, and follow the typical form of a leader's call and group response, with the drum maintaining a triple division of the basic pulse, while the singers periodically use a duple division—resulting in a "three-against-two" effect. Sometimes the songs include English lyrics, but not always.

In some forms, the round dance has ceremonial significance, but, in the modern pow-wow it is often performed as a social dance with individuals adding any personal, or religious significance mentally while performing. Some evidence indicates that many tribes used a round dance as the basic movement of the Ghost Dance (although the Ghost Dance was used to induce a trancelike state in which visions of the spirit world were received. Also, special regalia and preliminary ceremonies were associated with the Ghost Dance as performed in the late 1800s. See "Guided Listening Experience 6: *Ghost Dance*" for additional information about the Ghost Dance movement).

The round dance melodies originating at Taos Pueblo in the 1930s are considered the models for modern round dance tunes. Each tribe, naturally, performs these tunes in their regional styles and creates new songs based on these models. A typical round dance form includes a lead section in which the soloist indicates what song is to be performed, a second lead in which the entire group repeats the lead, a chorus either in vocables or tribal language—English is commonly used in many round dance songs—and repeats of the entire song. Other stylistic features include specially accented honor beats, and use of humor.

The lyrics of many social dance songs express sentiments similar to those found in any culture's popular music: love, tragedy, drinking. The lyrics to one song, "Even though we're married to someone else, we belong to each other tonight," could as easily come from Nashville as from the reservation.

There are as many versions of the round dance steps as there are groups performing the dance. In an intertribal pow-wow, several versions may be performed together or parts of several versions may be incorporated into one dance. While the majority of the participants will move clockwise, individuals from specific tribes or who are fulfilling a vow may dance in a counterclockwise movement around the main circle.

This dance is a variation of the round dance performed at many intertribal pow-wows. It is a social dance and is an important part of courtship.

DANCE INSTRUCTIONS:

The version below was observed at Window Rock, Navajo Nation •June, 1989.

• Dancers form a line alternating male and female (usually a "couple") facing forward with feet parallel.

• The line follows the lead couple in dancing clockwise, forming a circle. The left foot moves first with the right foot brought parallel with a side-stepping movement. There is less "lift" to the movement of the right foot. [In the Plains style, the right foot moves to a weaker beat pattern: ♪♪ ♪♪

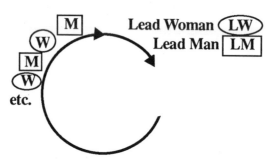

• At some point, the lead dancers will break the circle and move back down the line shaking hands with each dancer. Subsequent dancers imitate the lead dancers. The circle is rejoined after the lead dancer has greeted the last dancer. [This phase of the dance is an expression of friendship and peace among all participants.]

DANCE VARIATIONS:

In addition to the sidestepping movement described above, some variations commonly performed include:

• Simple "ring around the rosie" style with joined hands and a forward movement with both feet.

• Follow the leader, single file line, moving forward without joined hands, with or without specific hand/arm movements.

• Sidestepping, without joined hands, but with special upward and downward hand movements as if in supplication.

- More complex movement using alternating foot placement: (similar to a modified "grape-vine" step):

(Begin with feet parallel.)

Step one: left foot moves straight to side

Step two: right foot crosses to directly in front of left foot

Step three: left foot again moves out

Step four: right foot crosses to directly behind left foot

Hands are joined and move up and down in rhythm...up, two, down, four, etc.

PUEBLO ROUND DANCE

PUEBLO ROUND DANCE

OBSERVED: Pueblo Ysleta del Sur, in the Yselta section of El Paso; late 1980s to present; many variants.

GROUP: Pueblo Ysleta del Sur youth dancers

RECORDING: "Pueblo Ysleta Round Dance" or "Intertribal Dance" included in the following pages and on the recording, or any recorded round dance.

BACKGROUND:

Round dances are common to all tribes and are adapted by each group to conform to stylistic preferences. This round dance uses a "straight" beat drum accompaniment in contrast to some round dances from northern New Mexico which use syncopated drumming. Also, the step used is the cross-step pattern:

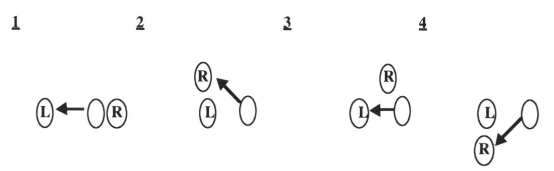

The introduction serves to announce the dance and allow dancers to take a starting position. Frequently, dancers are inviting members of the audience to participate in the dance and the pause before the main body of the song may be extended or the time filled with swirling the rattles and a repetitive beating of the drum.

Dancers move in a clockwise direction using the cross-step pattern described above with joined hands moving up and down to the beat. The direction of movement changes with each repeat of the verse.

INTERTRIBAL DANCE

INTERTRIBAL DANCE

OBSERVED: Baltimore Pow-Wow, 1990, '91, '92; frequently heard at east coast and Canadian pow-wows, with minor differences.

GROUP: Mid-Atlantic. Mixed group of whoever chose to take part around the drum. This song was chosen for the group to sing because it was known to everyone present.

RECORDING: "Intertribal Dance" on companion tape

BACKGROUND:

This song is representative of the modern intertribal style popular at pow-wows. The style of song is derived from the Plains traditions, but the vocal style is influenced by the tribal preference of the performing group. Because of the widespread usage of this tune, lyrics vary considerably from performance to performance. Sometimes only vocables will be used with even the choice of vocables determined by the performing group's preference while at other times lyrics in the language of the performing group may be used. The version given here is popular in the mid-Atlantic region. Over the years, I have heard it sung in many versions at the Baltimore Pow-Wow, which is typically held late in November of each year, coinciding with Thanksgiving weekend.

The function of this particular song also varies according to performer preference. It may be used as a grand entry song at a pow-wow when all dancers and dignitaries formally enter the arena for opening ceremonies. Dancers are grouped by type and each group enters dancing its particular style. It is truly an inspiring spectacle.

At a less formal gathering, an intertribal song may simply be used to get everyone dancing regardless of style (traditional, fancy, jingle, shawl, etc.). Dancers may or may not group themselves by style—grouping by family, friends, or tribe is not uncommon. On occasion, an intertribal song may be used as a specific type of social dance, e.g. Round Dance, Two-Step, or Forty-Niner, particularly if the singers come from different drums and need to use commonly-known songs for performance. The modern pow-wow includes many tribal styles, but because of many years of contact, a blending has begun to take place where the stylistic edges blur, and what is known as the pan-Indian style is common.

ZUNI POTTERY DANCE

ZUNI POTTERY DANCE

OBSERVED: Four corners region, New Mexico, Arizona, Utah, Colorado, 1989-91 several performances

GROUP: Non-professional Zuni women of various ages

RECORDING: "Pottery Dance" on companion tape

BACKGROUND:

Many dances from the Pueblo peoples consist of a number of shorter sections, often with contrasting styles and separated by improvisatory sections of singing. Examples of this include the various Hopi dances and the White Buffalo Dance performed by the Acoma Intercultural Dancers. (The Zuni, Hopi and Acoma are separate groups who are geographically close. Sometimes members of one group perform with those of another, particularly when there is repertoire in common.)

The Zuni Pottery Dance also fits this extended format. Young women of the pueblo perform a graceful dance to each section of the music while each woman balances an olla (oy-ah), a kind of pottery water jar, on her head. The simplest part of the dance consists of simply circling around the dance area showing grace and pride in movement. (This part sometimes takes place before the singing begins.) Each succeeding section increases in complexity of dance step and body movement. The Pottery Dance teaches the young women a needed skill—carrying water from the wells or springs back to the village—much in the same way the Hopi use the Corn Grinding Dance to teach younger members of the tribe a survival skill.

DANCE INSTRUCTIONS:

Because of the length and complexity of the dance, only a section is presented here. Each dancer balances a large olla on her head and holds flowers or small evergreen sprigs in each hand (the symbolism of flowers representing fertility is common throughout the southwest). One step is taken to each beat, the hands swing back and forth across the front of the body on each beat, a slight bounce may be detected on the half-beat pulses. Note that the hands move in the direction opposite from the foot movement—i.e., the hands swing to the left when the right foot moves forward and vice-versa (this movement aids in maintaining balance). When the dancers reach the end of the dance area, they turn around and move to the other end and prepare for more complex sections of the dance. Each step has a little springy rebound in it.

In the classroom, papier-mache bowls or soft plastic bowls should be substituted for the pottery jars.

BASKET DANCE

BASKET DANCE

OBSERVED: Pueblo Ysleta Del Sur, (in the Ysleta section of El Paso) Texas; August, 1989.

GROUP: Pueblo Ysleta del Sur dancers.

RECORDING: "Basket Dance" on the companion tape.

BACKGROUND:

Thanksgiving celebrations have always been a part of Native American culture. Whether celebrating a successful hunt or giving thanks for a bountiful harvest, the Native American acknowledged the gifts from Mother Earth.

These celebrations frequently occurred following the fall harvest and included days of ceremonial dancing and feasting. People of the village invited all friends and relatives to share in their abundance and join in the thanksgiving festivities. It is from these Native American celebrations that the American tradition of Thanksgiving grew—in the fall of 1621, Original Americans and New Americans sat down together in Plymouth Colony to celebrate and share the bounties of the Earth and give thanks to the Creator.

The Basket Dance is a harvest dance. Young women perform this dance carrying shallow baskets of corn or beans as part of the thanksgiving celebration. The symbolism of using young maidens (past puberty, yet not having borne children) is that of having the future of the tribe (represented by young, fertile maidens who bear the promise of generations to come) offer thanks for the present bounty granted because of the efforts of the past (older tribal members).

The actions portrayed in the dance imitate part of the harvest activities: the baskets are shaken so that the beans or ears of corn are tossed and "trash" materials are separated from the good. In this way, young children are taught both a useful skill and to celebrate the result of successful work for the tribe. (A similar function is served by the numerous corn grinding songs.)

DANCE INSTRUCTIONS:

During the introductory recitative-like section, four dancers take their places, one at each primary point of the compass, at a pre-determined distance from the center:

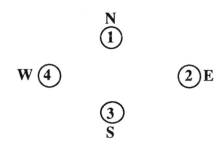

• During the first performance of the verse section, the women advance to the center of the dance floor while shaking their baskets to the beat of the drum; they face the center:

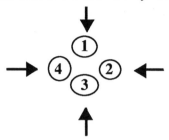

• Once at the center, the dancers take tiny steps to the side in a rotating, clockwise direction; this leaves them facing out, away from the center:

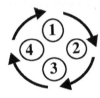

• When the "recitative" is repeated, dancers move from the center of the arena, shifting to the next point of the compass:

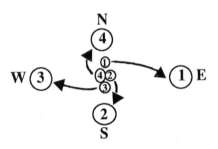

• This procedure continues until the dancers return to the starting position for the dance. (This final move is completed to a final statement of the "recitative.")

NANTICOKE WOMEN'S SHAWL DANCE

OBSERVED: Several East Coast cultural fairs and pow-wows 1991-92

GROUP: Mixed group from a special performance

RECORDING: "Nanticoke Shawl Dance" field recording on the companion tape

BACKGROUND:

As early as the 1580s, English and Spanish exploring the Chesapeake Bay area encountered the Nanticoke living in a number of villages along the Nanticoke River in an area of present-day Delaware and Maryland. In 1642, the Nanticoke were declared "enemies of the colony" by Maryland, and warfare between the whites and native people continued until 1742, with brief periods of peace following each of five treaties. Each treaty, however, failed to guarantee the Nanticokes' right to land ownership, and tribal holdings dwindled as white settlers continually encroached upon Nanticoke land. Following the Treaty of 1742, many Nanticoke families left the Delaware/Maryland area, moving first to Pennsylvania and then settling in New York, where they were adopted by the Iroquois League under the protection of the Cayuga. In the 1780s, other families moved to the Midwest where they became allies of the displaced Delaware.

A small number of families, however, remained on traditional Nanticoke land in southern Delaware and Maryland's eastern shore. They eventually lost government recognition as a tribe, found themselves classified as "free colored," and suffered humiliating discrimination. (Many smaller Mid-Atlantic tribes, including the Meherrin, the Waccamaw, Coharie, and Cheraw suffered a similar fate: they were forced to abandon their Native American identity in order to remain on their own land rather than be removed to Indian Territory. Some state governments still regard these groups as "of mixed ancestry" and refuse to recognize their rights as Native Americans. The Lumbees, for example, are the largest tribe east of the Mississippi, yet have state but not federal recognition. In North Carolina many of the smaller tribes have banded together to create an Indian cultural center for the lesser-known tribes, just outside Pembroke. Pembroke State University originated as an Indian school, run for the purpose of tribal education. (It evolved over the years into its current form of a University.) During the Twentieth Century, these families worked to reestablish tribal identity and to preserve the Nanticoke culture. Nanticoke actively participate in intertribal cultural fairs and pow-wows throughout the East Coast and host an annual pow-wow in rural Sussex County, Delaware. Typical of many contemporary tribes, the young, educated members are returning to work for the tribe rather than seeking employment in urban professions, taking on leadership positions to help guide their community.

The Women's Shawl Dance of the Nanticoke is not to be confused with the Fancy Shawl Dance commonly performed at pow-wows and tribal fairs. (The fancy dance is descended from a form of the Butterfly dance in which the dancers "emerge" from the cocoon of the shawl, transformed into a graceful butterfly.) It is one of the few surviving original East Coast style dances, with dancers learning from other dancers, always referring to the Nanticoke as the source. Sometimes referred to as the Swan Dance, this dance features beautiful shawls used to imitate the gracefulness of birds with movements mimicking soaring, gliding, and flying. The bowing of heads and lowering of shawls signifies humility before the Creator, while the movement of the dance honors the four directions.

In a typical performance of the Shawl Dance, women dancers follow a lead dancer into the circle with arms extended and shawls flowing to represent wings. The tilt of the arms with the shawl outspread shows various stages of flight. Dancers freely use motions of soaring, gliding, slow flapping, and graceful body movements to honor birds through imitation. At some point, the dancers form two rows and the lead pair weaves through the group—"soaring" and "gliding"—with subsequent pairs beginning this movement at the point where the maneuver was initiated by the lead dancer. Eventually, the dancers follow the lead dancer out of the dance circle. As with many Native American dances, the exact sequence of movements is flexible depending upon the lead dancer and creativity of individual dancers.

DANCE INSTRUCTIONS:

Although the exact movements of the dance rely upon a lead dancer, the Shawl Dance usually follows the following format:

1. Dancers enter the dance circle and follow the lead dancer using a serpentine path to the center. (Note: throughout the dance, the left foot takes a full step, leaving the ground while the right foot maintains contact with the earth and rapidly slides into place on the proper beat, giving the dancers an almost limping appearance).

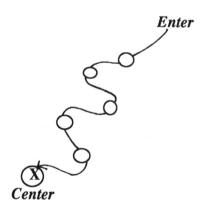

2. Dancers are led to face each of the four directions by the lead dancer, again using the serpentine path.

• **A.** The dancers move to form a single line to face the first direction (A-1). The lead dancer then weaves through the line with each dancer following suit (A-2).

A-1:   **A-2:**

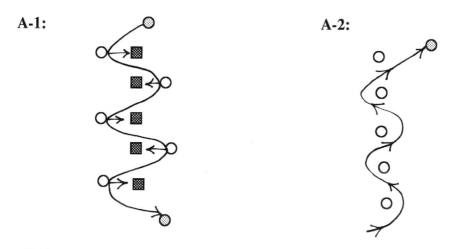

• **B.** A single file is formed and the dancers follow the leader to face the second direction. The line then breaks into two lines through a side-stepping motion (B-1). Then the lead dancer weaves between the two lines (B-2) and leads the dancers to the third direction, using the same sequence as for the first direction) and then the fourth direction (using the same sequence as for the second direction).

B-1:   **B-2:**

3. After each direction has been honored, the lead dancer leads the group to form a circle in the center of the dance area (symbolizing the center of the universe). The dancers continue to move in this circle until the end of the current repetition of the song (3-A). At this point, the dancers face the center of the circle and lower heads and upper bodies in a symbol of respect to the universe and all living things. (Drums may continue to "roll" or tremolo at this point.) When the singing resumes, the dancers follow the lead dancer through the circle and exit the dance area (3-B).

3-A: **3-B:**

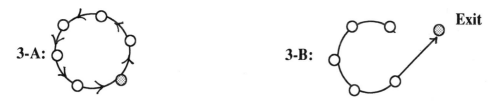

NANTICOKE WOMEN'S SHAWL DANCE

INDIAN TWO-STEP

OBSERVED: Recorded version observed at Pueblo Ysleta Del Sur, in the Ysleta section of El Paso, 1989.

GROUP: Tigua Pueblo. The Tigua are the descendants of Pueblo Indians who remained loyal to the Spanish and Catholic Church followed the great Pueblo Revolt in 1681. The Spanish and loyalist tribes moved from the original Isleta location (near present day Albuquerque) to a new site on the south bank of the Rio Grande near modern Ciudad Juarez. Changes in the course of the Rio Grande eventually placed the tribal lands in the United States. The Tigua almost lost their identity as Native Americans completely through absorption into the Mexican-American community. Many years of effort were rewarded with both state and federal recognition of the tribe's identity. The tribe operates a cultural center and crafts-oriented business enterprise.

RECORDING: "Two-Step," on the companion tape, performed by young Tigua dancers; or any social dance/round dance.

BACKGROUND:

The "Indian Two-Step" originated during the period when performance of "authentic" dances was prohibited by Federal law. The Two-Step was permitted as it appeared to copy a "white man's dance." (The Native Americans, however, sometimes used the "acceptable" dances, but continued other rituals associated with dances "out of the white man's sight." One older performer told me that the white man could change the outward appearance of the dance, but could not change the more important inner thoughts and beliefs.) Several theories have been put forward regarding the origin of the steps themselves. A popular version credits Native American veterans returning from World War I with bringing some of the currently popular dance steps from the non-Indian world back to the reservations. Another belief is that Native Americans copied the dances of white settlers they observed at community social functions. There is, however, evidence of similar dances in Native American traditions dating back to the early 1800s—clog dancing reputedly incorporates some steps from traditional Cherokee dancing.

The Two-Step may have been a variation of the Rabbit Dance, another highly popular couple dance possibly originating in the West. (One informant states the "limping" step of the Rabbit Dance caused a dragging footprint similar to the track left by a rabbit.) The Rabbit Dance, and other couple dances, were responsible for many marital problems as it was a woman's choice dance—the woman chose her partner even if the partner was married to someone else. Although it was an honor to have one's husband chosen, the fact was that jealousies arose and created many difficulties in Native life. In general, men and women do not dance as couples in the traditional dances. Since choosing a partner during a "ladies' choice" dance might indicate more than passing interest in the man, just to be safe or to avoid controversy some women will choose a relative or a boy. The humorous lyrics of the Rabbit Dance—often relating to philandering or flirtation—have continued in the modern Two-Step, Round Dance, and Forty-Niner Dance. (For more on the Rabbit Dance and its possible origins, see the next selection, Iroquois Rabbit Dance "Uncle Sam.") Whatever the origin of the "Indian Two-Step," it has become one of the most popular and widespread dances performed by Native Americans today.

The titles of some of the currently popular dance songs reflect the continuation of the humorous lyrics tradition: "One-eyed Ford" ("When the dance is over, sweetheart, I will take you home in my one-eyed Ford."); "The Rolls Songs" ("Honey, dear, I love you so even though you've got the rolls and your clothes don't fit just right."); "One-Night Stand"; "This Bud's For You," etc. The songs

77

frequently employ some English words as a "lingua franca" among all tribes with alternating verses in a tribal language or in vocables or any combination of languages. As with any popular music (of any culture), the same popular songs may be used to accompany a variety of dance steps.

DANCE INSTRUCTIONS:

The Two-Step resembles, in many ways, the Virginia Reel or other types of square dancing. A lead couple replaces the caller of the square dance and set the movements of the dance by their example. Following couples perform the same movements when reaching the point at which the lead couple executed the move. The instructions below include only a minute number of possibilities for the Two-Step. The exact form the dance takes depends upon the skill and imagination of the lead couple. A dance may evolve from Two-Step to Round Dance to Snake Dance and back many times during a performance. As with any Native American Dance, great flexibility is allowed individuals in their interpretation of the movements. Some tribal cultural centers sponsor Two-Step teams who perform in matched dance outfits at inter-tribal competitions. This, again, is similar to the square dance phenomenon of the white culture.

A line of couples is formed behind a lead dance couple. The male dancer stands to the left of the female. The couple holds hands "skater style," i.e., left hand holding left, right hand holding right (see photo of the Haliwa-Saponi dancers below the musical transcription).

Forward movement begins with the left foot. The left foot is lifted higher than the right in a slightly shuffling step. [Some variations use a "two steps forward, one step back" basic sequence.]

BASIC MOVEMENTS:

1. Basic Circle: Couples follow the lead couple in a large clockwise circle of the dance floor returning to the point of origin.

2. Split circle: Lead couple splits with male moving counterclockwise around half of the dance floor, while the female moves clockwise around half the dance floor. Subsequent couples imitate the lead couple. Couples rejoin upon meeting.

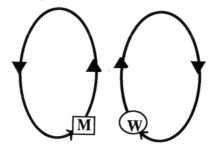

3. Arch: The lead couple faces and forms an arch with joined hands. Subsequent couples pass under the arch and form their own arch.

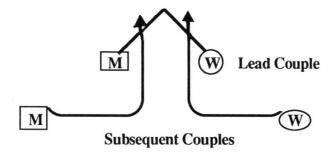

When all couples have formed an arch, the lead couple rejoins and goes under the arch. Subsequent couples imitate the lead couple, moving under the arch until the original dance line has been reformed.

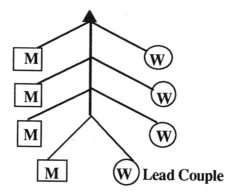

4. Popular variations:

• *Twirl* ("Jitterbug"): Dancers drop the left hand continuing to hold right hands. The male does a basic step in place while the female tightly circles in a clockwise direction. The hands are held above the head.

• *Spin:* While continuing to hold hands, each couple executes this movement:

Male moves in large clockwise circle around the female dancer while the female dancer moves in a tight clockwise circle in place.

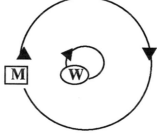

• *Push Dance:* One or both of the dancers in the couple reverses and dances "backwards" for a set length of time. This variation is quite popular among the Crow among whom it may have originated.

PUEBLO TWO-STEP

Rattles:
Drum:

Intro.

Voice: Ya he ne yo - a he ne ya he ne yo - e na. Ya he ne yo - a

he ne ya hene yo - e na he ne ya yo hene ya - a he ya he - e-

e- e ya. He - e-a he-e-a he-e yo-o yo e yo a -he -ya e

he - e ya ya ne o yo he ne yo-a he ya he - e - e - e ya.

The Two-Step, showing the "skater's handhold" as danced by
the Haliwa-Saponi Dancers.

RABBIT DANCE: "UNCLE SAM"
FLUTE VERSION, SOUTH DAKOTA

RABBIT DANCE: "UNCLE SAM"

Voice

He - e he - he ya he   hea hea   he-ya e   he - he - he ya he

Drum, Rattles

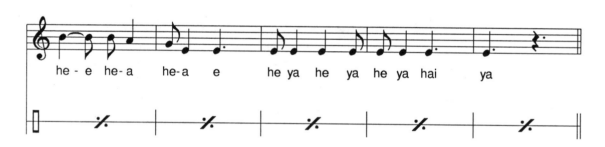

he - e he-a   he-a   e   he ya he ya he ya hai   ya

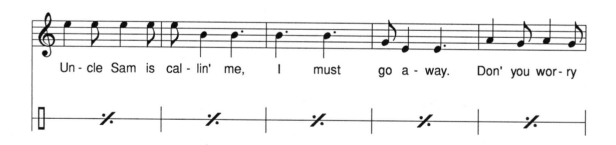

Un - cle Sam is cal - lin' me,   I   must   go a - way.   Don' you wor - ry

don' you cry   I'll be home - by 'n' by.   he ya he ya he ya hai   ya.

82

RABBIT DANCE: "UNCLE SAM"

SOURCE: Learned from elderly Seneca singer, western NY, 1989

GROUP: Seneca (Iroquois) of New York. Several reservations continue to exist in New York and on the Pennsylvania border in Allegany County, including the Tonawanda, Cattaraugus, and Allegany Reservations, and a number of Iroquois reserves may be found in Canada. The Seneca Nation includes the Allegany and Cattaraugus Senecas; the Tonawanda Band of Senecas is politically separate.

RECORDING: Rabbit Dance: "Uncle Sam" sung by Seneca man using dance bells and bone rattle; Flute version: South Dakota, both on companion recording.

BACKGROUND:

Historically, tribes of the Iroquois Confederacy occupied the lake region and Mohawk Valley of New York State. Sometime between 1000 and 1450, the warring Oneida, Seneca, Onondaga, Cayuga, and Mohawk tribes were united in a confederacy by Dekanawida and Hiawatha under a constitution known as the Great Law of Peace. (The Tuscarora joined after 1715 and were given part of the Oneida lands.) The strength of the united tribes gave the Iroquois League the dominant position in the northeast woodlands region in matters of trade and warfare. The Iroquois achieved the highest form of governmental organization of any people north of the Valley of Mexico. Following the American Revolution, many members of the tribes moved to Ontario, and tribal lands within the United States shrank to only a fraction of their original size.

The present structure of the United States government is modelled in great part on the Iroquois League. As early as 1744 at a meeting between representatives of the English colonies and Native Americans, the Iroquois leader Canassatego recommended that the colonies unite in a league similar to that formed by the Iroquois. Benjamin Franklin, who as printer for the Colony of Pennsylvania was familiar with speeches by Native leaders and was a student of Native life, recommended to the 1754 Congress of Albany that the colonies form a union based on the Iroquois model. Some three decades later, the writers of the Constitution based many facets of the new United States government upon traditions of the Iroquois.

"Uncle Sam," the song presented here, is an Iroquois Rabbit Dance I learned from an older Seneca man who indicated that it had been very popular among his people, "When I was a young man about to go in the army." English lyrics are used for part of the song and help give a historical context—many Native Americans joined the armed forces during World Wars I and II as a means of earning warrior honors. The words "Uncle Sam is calling me," could be interpreted as meaning either that the man had received a draft notice, or had been drawn to volunteer. "We sang this song at rabbit dances to our sweethearts to make them feel sad that we were going away," my friend said. "Sometimes we got lucky. Same trick you whites used to pull on your girlfriends!"

For the taped version, the singer accompanied himself with dance bells and bone rattle rather than the water drum preferred by many Iroquois. The hoarse, strained vocal style may be attributed more to the age of the singer rather than traditional performance technique, which among the Iroquois singers tends to be more open than the style of the Plains and Southwest.

This song also demonstrates one of the difficulties of researching song origins in an oral/aural culture. Although this song was cited as being popular among the Senecas and therefore qualifying as an *Iroquois* Rabbit Dance, there are versions of the song found throughout the United States. A flute version of this melody learned from a South Dakota musician was identified as being an older popular social dance, "One my father liked a lot and said was sung around the 1940s." Here we have a similar tune from the same era, but in a locale many miles distant from the Seneca and performed by a different tribe.

Further complicating identification of the exact origin of the song is yet another version of the "Uncle Sam" theme I learned at a pow-wow in Texas. In this version, there are several differences in melodic line and some added textual phrases. The song is still recognizable as a variation of the Seneca tune. Such differences may easily be explained by the natural changes occurring when a song is transmitted by ear through a series of musicians over a several-year period. The "Uncle Sam is calling me" refrain appeared to be an "insert" into a series of verses from other songs related to courtship to make a longer song used to accompany a Two-Step (one of the descendants of the original Rabbit Dance).

Which version is the original? Making such a determination is most likely impossible. What may be determined is that a particular melody and vocal refrain gained wide popularity during the early 1940s and is still performed throughout the Native American culture today. In addition, we can see that this version of Uncle Sam follows the structure of the Plains social dance form, and the text appears to date from World War II, because of the subject matter. The original source for this version is this particular elderly Seneca man, who says the song is performed for Rabbit Dances.

The mystery deepens as we encounter Mary Reimer, who recorded and annotated the 1980 Folkways recording *Seneca Social Dance Songs* sung by Avery and Fidelia Jimerson, who lived in Salamanca near the Pennsylvania border. She quotes the Jimersons as saying Rabbit Dances were brought from "the West" to the Seneca at Allegany by Herb Dowdy in the early 1960s, after which Herb Dowdy and Avery Jimerson became composers of numerous Rabbit Dances used by the Seneca in that locale. Reginald Laubin, on the other hand, indicates the Seneca learned the Rabbit Dance in 1952 and discontinued the dance in 1958 because of social discontent. He believes the Seneca learned the dance from Lakota sources. Perhaps the tradition noted by Mary Reimer was evidence of a re-birth of the earlier waxing and waning of Rabbit Dances. Rabbit Dances are very popular social dances among the Iroquois in general. They are ladies' choice couple dances, with a pair of lead dancers determining the steps used in the dance. Lyrics combine vocables with humorous commentary on courtship. Because of the jealousies aroused at social dances (single women often selected married men as dance partners), the Rabbit Dance fell out of favor for many years, but is now regaining its former popularity on the pow-wow circuit. As with the Two-Step, it is not uncommon these days to see a woman dancing with her nephew or a male much younger than she is, to avoid controversy or misunderstandings.

There are perhaps as many versions given for the origin of the Rabbit Dance as there are tribes performing the dance. One strong theory is that it is derived from the Northern Plains Cree Rabbit Skin Wearers Dance. Another is that the Rabbit Dance is derived from the Lakota Kahomni dance, which was a women's dance resembling the Rabbit Dance. The limping step used was a women's dance step, and the dragging step indicated their connection with the earth. (The step-back seen on the East Coast is not a Lakota dance step.) It evolved into a women's choice social dance. Most tribes performing the dance today cite origins on the Plains, or they "learned it from the West;" both the Cree and Lakota would fit this description. The present day name and the dance adaptation popular among non-Indians probably came in the 1920s when some performers called it the Bunny Dance.

DANCE INSTRUCTIONS:

- Follow the instructions for the Indian Two-Step, using the "skater's" handhold.
- Use the Two-Step variation of two steps forward, followed by one step back, as the basic Rabbit Dance step for traveling in the large counterclockwise circle. The couple sometimes swing their linked arms forward and back rhythmically, dipping from the waist a bit on the back step.

"ONE-EYED FORD"

OBSERVED: Baltimore Intertribal pow-wow, 1991

GROUP: Mixed

RECORDING: *Round Dance Songs With English Lyrics,* Indian Sounds IS 1004; sung by Tom Mauchahty-Ware (Kiowa-Comanche) and Millard Clark (Cheyenne-Comanche). Other songs on this recording are representative of the humorous songs characteristic of the repertoire heard on the modern pow-wow circuit.

BACKGROUND:

"One-Eyed Ford" is typical of the modern intertribal social dance song in its use of English lyrics and in its reliance on the round dance form for musical structure. Although the dance is a round dance, it is sometimes played for a Two-Step or Rabbit Dance.

A lead singer sings a brief motif ("head") that identifies the song and is then joined by other singers who repeat this motif before the basic verse is performed in vocables. The verse is then sung using English. Some performances alternate verses in vocables, a Native American language (often Lakota), and English. The entire song is repeated as often as indicated by the lead singer. Honor beats—three or four accented drum beats—near the end of the verse are performed to honor an individual (usually no announcement is made of the honoree; however, Native Americans recognize the purpose). Some drummers use the accented beats as cues to dancers.

Another trait typical of the modern social dance song is the humor contained in the lyrics. The "One-Eyed Ford" is a reference to the condition of many cars on the reservations where state inspection and licensing laws are not enforced. An earlier version states, "I'll take you to the dance, sweetheart, in my new Model-T Ford."An even earlier generation sang a similar melody with the singer telling his sweetheart that he would "take her home in my manufactured wagon." Another source hinted that some versions once used "take you home on my best pony." This is an example of the lyrics in a popular song changing over time to accommodate advances in lifestyle.

As previously mentioned, songs travel from group to group and undergo changes based on regional style preferences. The transcription given here was made from a field tape recorded on the East Coast while the accompanying tape features a performance by two Oklahoma musicians. There are slight variations in rhythm, drum accompaniment, and vocables although the song is readily identifiable.

DANCE INSTRUCTIONS:

Any social dance such as the Two-Step, Rabbit or various styles of round dances may appropriately be used with this song.

"ONE-EYED FORD"

He ya he ne he ya he ya ya he-e ye
He ya he ne heye he ya

he ya he-e ya he yo hi ya he ya hi he ya hi ya. When the

dance is o-ver, sweetheart, I will take you home in my one eyed Ford. he ya

he ya yo he ya he ya hi - (u) he ya hi - (u)

CHAPTER **5**

SONGS OF THE WIND · THE NATIVE AMERICAN FLUTE

Photo on the previous page: R. Carlos Nakai, Navajo/Ute
flutist and educator, leader of the fusion group Jackalope.
 (Photo: © John Running)

LEGEND

Origin of the Indian Love Flute

A young man of the tribe deeply loved a beautiful young woman, but the woman showed no response to his advances and acted as if the man did not even exist. The man went to seek the advice of a holy man (medicine man) regarding how to win the love of his maiden. The holy man told him to find a tree which had recently been struck by lightening, make a flute from the branch where the lightening had struck, and return to him with the finished flute.

After the man returned, the holy man purified and blessed the new flute. The man was instructed to wait until the new moon and then play songs outside the tent of his beloved. Although impatient to win the maiden's love, he followed the holy man's instructions and waited until the new moon arose. The gentle breeze, the moonlight and his pure love inspired his playing. Many hours were spent playing newly-composed songs waiting for the maiden's response. When a cloud covered the new moon, the man worried that this was a bad omen and his ancestors did not intend for him to marry this woman.

However, when the cloud passed from the moon and the man resumed his songs, the maiden came out from her lodge and, opening the courting blanket, gestured for the man to join her. The songs from the flute had won her love for the man.

SONGS OF THE WIND
THE NATIVE AMERICAN FLUTE

Sometimes referred to as the "Indian Love Flute," the Native American Flute is the primary wind instrument of the Native American peoples. The instrument has its origins in courtship rituals among the Plains tribes and in some ceremonies in the southwestern United States and northwestern Mexico, and is now used to play virtually any type of Native American music including ceremonial as well as social styles. The story, "Origin of the Indian Love Flute," common among Plains tribes including the Lakota, Kiowa and Comanche, describes the origins of the flute as a courtship instrument.

Most often, the flute is constructed from wood or cane with a strong preference for cedar, considered sacred by many tribes. When making a wooden flute, two pieces of wood are first hollowed out. (A block of wood is left beneath the tone hole to force the wind through the "roost"—the carved depression—properly. *See illustration below.*) A carved animal usually referred to as the "bird" is placed in the roost over the tone hole to control tone quality. Some are quite decorative. (Birds —owl, loon, whippoorwill, eagle, meadowlark, quail—and other animals such as bear have been used, usually chosen because they have some significance to the maker.) Any metal or wooden base between the "roost" and the "bird" is termed the "nest." The carved animal is tied to the body of the flute with an elk hide or deer hide thong which allows adjustment for individual taste. Some placements allow a very pure tone, others produce a more breathy sound. Adjustable "birds" also facilitate tuning as the wood flute responds to humidity and temperature changes. Kiowa permanently attach the "bird" to the body of the flute and use a moveable flattened bullet to control tone. Before the two

LEGEND

The Story of the Woodpecker Flute

There was an Indian man on a horse, and he was riding by and noticed a woodpecker on a branch. He had that feeling we sometimes get that someone was trying to tell him something. So he got off his horse and walked over to the branch where the bird had been perched.

The bird flew away, but the woodpecker had pecked five holes in the branch. He broke the branch off the tree, and as he stood looking at it the wind rushed through it and made a sound. He took the branch back to the medicine man and asked him what this meant.

The medicine man said, "This is a gift from the Great Spirit. Take it, play it and win the heart of the woman who truly listens to it." From that day many of the courting flutes have their head in the shape of a woodpecker.

- Greg Borst,
Sing Out! 1976

halves of the flute are joined together with glue, three to six finger holes are carved, drilled, or burned in the upper section of wood.

Additional decorations may be carved or painted on the body of the flute. Often, "wind holes" are carved into the end of the flute to allow the songs to go to the four directions. Among northern plains tribes, the end of the flute is frequently carved into a bird's head or other animal form. Individuals may prefer to have their flute ritually cured (blessed) in a ceremony during which the flute is passed through scented smoke. Such flutes are then highly rubbed, giving a shining finish with smoke and burn marks somewhat evident. Well-known flute makers have distinctive styles of tuning, carving, decorating and finishing their flutes. On occasion a flute player will approach a particular artisan and commission a new flute of the crafter's choice. The old master artisans encouraged the player to stay a while in their village, to interact with them frequently. Their goal was to really know the player's personality, life-style and attitudes and thus unlock the key to what the best flute would be for that person. When I had one of my flutes made by such a maker, it was a joint effort to define what I was seeking, but I had the distinct feeling he understood better than I what would be right for me. Like guitar players who collect fine instruments and take great joy in playing them, many flute players build a treasure of flutes with varying sounds, scales, textures, woods, and design that bear the indelible stamp of their maker. Some make their own as part of an apprenticeship to the instrument.

Almost unbelievably, making and playing the traditional Native American flute had nearly become a lost art, with most flutes in museum collections. Doc Tate is an important figure in the renewal of this tradition, as he was given access to flutes stored in museums, and used his own breath and dedication to instill new interest in the instrument and its gentle power. Master flute makers currently making flutes include Doc Tate, Arnold Richardson (a spiritual leader of the Haliwa-Saponi of North Carolina), Todd Bear MacFarlane, and Dave Powell.

The design and size of the Native American flute is highly individualized as the instrument should match the singer's voice and songs. (Lengths of the flutes in the photos seen here vary from six to twenty-four inches with from three to six holes used to produce notes.) There are various guidelines for creating the proper flute for a musician. One traditional set of measurements for a Native American flute suggests that the length should be from the singer's elbow to the fingertips; the tone hole should be one hand width from the tip of the flute; the first finger hole should be a hand width from the tone hole; finger holes should be spaced using thumb widths and "half thumb" widths to set the "tuning;" finger holes should be approximately the width of the little finger; the diameter of the opening at the bottom of the flute should be the length of the tip to first knuckle of the index finger.

The scale on a Native American flute only approximates the pitches in traditional western music. Songs notated in Western notation reflect neither the variance from standard tuning nor the elaborate systems of ornamentation including pitch bending, tremolos (shakes), and portamenti (slides) common to Native American musics. One common tuning used on commercially available flutes approximates the following scale:

LEGEND

The Story of the Orphan Boy

Once there was an orphan boy who had few friends. He wandered through the woodlands seeking companionship among the animals and plants of the forest.

One day, he heard a voice - that of the Creator - calling to him. The voice said, "Go find a tree and cut a branch about so long." When the boy had cut the branch, he was told how to carve it into a flute. A carved bird was placed over a tone hole and other animals and symbols were carved and painted onto the child's now beautiful instrument.

"Take your songs from nature," The Creator told the orphan, "and you will always have good music." The Orphan copied the sounds of the wind and the trees and imitated the songs of the birds. His music gained him the respect and friendship of many people.

Because of the open tone quality, the gentle, almost meditative melodies, the presence of sounds imitative of nature in the songs, and performances recorded outdoors, the Native American flute has become quite popular among New Age Music followers. Native American recordings often include real (or synthesized) sounds of rain, thunder, water running, bird calls, fire crackling, and insect sounds. This parallels usage in New Age recordings. Frequently, record stores will place Native American music—especially flute music—in the New Age bin, and buyers report using the recordings as aids to meditation and relaxation.

One Native American flutist has commented, "New Age? My people have been playing this way for hundreds of years!" Somewhat less cynical performers are proud that music from their culture is beginning to reach a wider audience and are producing recordings specifically designed for the New Age market.

The traditional story on this page provides a possible origin for using the sounds of nature in Native American music: In some communities, young men and women use cupped hands for whistling special phrases that signal arrangements for meetings. In others, a young man will play his songs near where his love is gathering berries, or washing clothes at the river, or near his girlfriend's home in the evening, trying to entice her out for a visit, or to make her feel lonely for him. Some of the flute songs have words that may be sung as well as, or even instead of, played. John Bierhorst, in *A Cry From the Earth*, includes a Pima song recorded in 1927 that says, "I play my flute and shake her heart. Oh, when the sun goes down, I make my flowers bloom, I shake her heart." (p.81) One loon-head flute made by Todd Bear MacFarlane is in keeping with the idea of a courting flute—it is very soft, sweet and gentle, requiring the listener to be very close to the player. In general, only men play the flute.

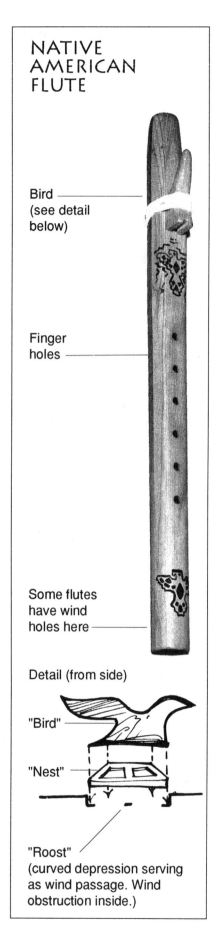

NATIVE AMERICAN FLUTE

Bird
(see detail
below)

Finger
holes

Some flutes
have wind
holes here

Detail (from side)

"Bird"

"Nest"

"Roost"
(curved depression serving
as wind passage. Wind
obstruction inside.)

PLAYING THE NATIVE AMERICAN FLUTE

"There's no way to teach the Indian flute, you just have to learn it yourself," said flute maker Doc Tate in an interview in Oklahoma Today (1984). Fernando Cellición has said that the songs already exist—the player simply begins, and then catches or remembers them. Playing melodies on the Native American flute is similar to playing on a recorder. The flute is held vertically. Air is gently blown—avoid overblowing—into the top of the instrument, while covering and uncovering finger holes creates the pitches. Because of the uniqueness of each instrument, however, it may not be possible to play all songs or a particular song on some flutes. A performer will usually own several flutes in order to play a wider repertoire. Flutes with a more completely diatonic scale are available from companies specializing in ethnic instruments (House of Musical Traditions, Tacoma Park, Maryland, for example) with cross fingerings used to create accidentals. An easy-to-assemble flute kit is now marketed by Steve Eagle's (see Appendix), providing a serviceable flute for under twenty dollars. Canyon Records and Indian Arts now carries a hand-made wood flute for under $80 that comes with a brief instruction booklet. Canyon also carries tapes and books of instruction and repertoire.

Simple transcriptions, as are included in this section, are accessible even to the novice. Ornamentation is essential, however, if the music is to sound more authentic. Simple techniques, such as ascending grace notes (where a lower finger is quickly lifted up), descending grace notes (requiring a finger to be hammered-down), free mordents (wiggling of the fingers over random holes, a movement similar to "drumming" the fingers before settling on the sustained pitch), and tremolos add to the flavor of Native American music. Grace notes are played somewhat more slowly than might be typical in other music, lingering on the first pitch before moving to the primary note. Portamenti (swoops, slurs and slides) between notes are common in Native American songs and may be readily performed by simply lifting fingers slowly while bending the pitch by air pressure or embouchure manipulation.

The "flutter" heard in many flute recordings is produced by rapidly pulsing air through the flute and is indicated in notation as: 〜 ....

The best way to understand how to use ornamentation is to listen to performances by such artists as R. Carlos Nakai (Navajo-Ute who has studied with many players from other traditions and plays traditional pieces as well as his own "fusion" compositions in collaboration with other musicians);

LISTEN

Absorb the style

1. Listen to the recordings and absorb the individual style while following the transcriptions.
2. Play each piece by ear or from the transcription with no ornamentation.
3. If your flute or recorder is in tune with that on the recording, play along.
4. Play again, this time attempt simple embellishments.
5. As confidence develops and expertise grows, weave in more improvisation and ornamentation.

John Rainer, Jr. (an educator, flute maker, and intertribal choir director from Taos Pueblo); Kevin Locke (a Lakota player, singer and dancer with a great sense of humor whose flute playing is heard in *Dances With Wolves*); Fernando Cellición (a Zuni who works with the Zuni public schools, travels as a member of traditional Zuni dance groups as well as a solo flute performer); Tom Mauchahty-Ware (a multi-faceted Kiowa-Comanche singer, dancer and drum player); Robert Tree Cody (of Dakota-Maricopa heritage, he is also a dancer and teacher of Indian crafts). There are many other players performing and recording today. Each is thoroughly versed in authentic performance techniques appropriate to the tribal music being performed. The companion tape gives you an introduction to the flute, and the discography offers more exposure to these widely-respected musicians. Beginning flute players generally learn by listening to and imitating more experienced players. This has been primarily an oral/aural tradition, although some notated examples of flute pieces do exist, transcribed from the playing of turn-of-the-century performers. (See Natalie Curtis, *The Indians' Book,* Frances Densmore's collections, *Music of the Native North American for Flute and Recorder* transcribed by Daniel Chazanoff, or *A Cry From the Earth* by John Bierhorst.)

Each of the selections here should first be performed as written without ornamentation. Younger players might try drumming the fingers, or slowly lifting them off or placing them over the holes. More experienced and confident performers might experiment with a variety of ornaments as heard on recordings by Native American flutists. The ultimate goal of any performer on the Native American flute is to be able to improvise songs in true Native American style, moving toward a very personal expression for one's own enjoyment of the sound coming through the player. Do not force this process; be receptive, linger patiently, explore the sound palette. (These songs have all been transcribed so that they will be easily playable on soprano or alto recorders.)

PUEBLO SUNRISE SONG AND "CALL TO SUNRISE"

ZUNI

I learned these two songs in western New Mexico from Zuni musicians. Sunrise songs are performed early in the morning to welcome the sun and to thank the sun for returning another day and giving life to all things upon the Earth. Zuni Pueblo first had contact with European culture in the early 1500s when explorers seeking the Cities of Cibola visited Zuni villages. Estebano, a Moorish slave who was eventually killed, sent word to Fray Marcos that he had discovered a city of gold at Zuni. Marcos reported that he saw the sun reflected from buildings of gold when viewing Zuni from a distance. Coronado's expedition sought this golden city at Zuni, but was disappointed to find only mud buildings with mica flecks reflecting the sunlight.

Although Zuni was "conquered" by Coronado, efforts to convert the Zuni people to Christianity failed and missions were withdrawn. Despite nearly five hundred years of contact with European culture, the Zuni remained faithful to their traditional beliefs and have continued to practice their rituals and ceremonies based on these traditions to the present time. The Zuni continue to live on the lands where they were first encountered by the Spanish explorers, and have maintained their musical and artistic culture and unique language (related to no other language on earth).

"Call to Sunrise" is a transcription of one of the most popular of all Native American tunes. According to ethnomusicologist David McAllester, the anthropologist Frank Hamilton Cushing learned this song after he was adopted into the Zuni tribe, around the turn of the century. He shared it with other researchers and musicians, and it was eventually issued as sheet music, used in movie scores, and found its way into various collections and repertoires. The song continued to be passed down within the Zuni community in the traditional way. Versions appear on at least ten commercial recordings of Native American music ranging from a simple presentation by Chester Mahooty (*Music from Zuni Pueblo* on the Tribal Music International label) to an elaborately orchestrated performance by John Rainer, Jr. (*Songs of the Indian Flute, Volume 2* from Red Willow Songs). Recorded versions include both solo flute and vocal performances of this song.

Contemporary composer James DeMars used "Call to Sunrise" in his works *Spirit Horses* and *Premonitions of Christopher Columbus*. Both works were composed for and feature R. Carlos Nakai performing on Native American flute accompanied by chamber orchestra. (A recording of *Spirit Horses* is available from Canyon Records.)

"CALL TO SUNRISE"

COURTING SONG

Sometimes called "Wedding Song," this is a song from the Lakota people of the northern Plains. Among the Plains communities, the cedar flute (*wi'ikizho* in the Dakota language) developed as an important instrument to be used in the courtship rituals of young people (see stories above). The Dakota, Lakota and Nakota peoples (named according to the dialects they speak, whether Santee, Teton or Yankton) are one of the largest tribes. The Pine Ridge, Rosebud and Standing Rock Reservations are among the largest of the many areas where Lakota live in South Dakota, but other groups also live on the Fort Totten Reservation in eastern North Dakota, Fort Peck in northeastern Montana and even in Minnesota. The song presented here is frequently performed at weddings among Lakota people in the states of North and South Dakota and a version appears in the musical score for the movie *A Man Called Horse*. This song is sometimes used in performances of the "Ribbon Dance." Using three long colored ribbons—red representing Man, blue representing the Creator, and yellow representing Woman - three couples dance with subtle movements and patterns that weave the ribbons into a braid. Braiding the ribbons represents the forces working together for the good of the tribe. When the braid is complete, the dancers reverse directions, unbraiding the ribbons until they are separate again. This represents individuality and freedom, the responsibility each person holds for making choices without disrespecting others. The dance continues as the ribbons are rolled into a bundle, which is returned by the man to the woman as a sign of her final authority - a reflection of the matriarchal society of the Lakota. A version of this song may be found in *The Indians' Book* by Natalie Curtis. The words are: Inkpataya nawazhin (up the creek I stand and wave), na shina cicoze (see, all alone I wave!), ma-ya, ma-ya (come here, come here), Lechiya ku wanna! (quickly to me). (Similar words are also noted in *American Indian Music for the Classroom* by Louis Ballard.)

COURTING SONG ORNAMENTS:

LOVE SONG

KIOWA

This is another courting song from the Plains tradition. I learned it in Arizona from a player who had learned it from a Kiowa performer. It is most likely Kiowa in origin. The Kiowa originally lived as nomadic hunters (particularly of buffalo) in the area around the sources of the Missouri and the Yellowstone rivers. In 1867 they were settled with the Comanches in the territory that later became Oklahoma. A large number live in the Anadarko and Carnegie area of southwestern Oklahoma. The Kiowa believe they were the first people given the traditional flute. An old Library of Congress recording (L39) features a person speaking in Kiowa about the origin of a particular flute song which is then played. This is one of the oldest recordings known of Native American flute music. The Kiowa used the flute for healing, both spiritual/mental and physical healing, as well as courtship. Only certain old masters knew the healing repertoire, and unfortunately, in many cases they died without passing on their legacy of songs to younger players. Since the 1940s and 1950s Kiowa and Kiowa/Comanche players like Doc Tate and Tom Ware have helped to revive interest in the flute through their own intense dedication to the instrument. Whether as master flute makers, players, channels for new melodies or teachers, the commitment to breathe new life into this important tradition has benefited us all and sparked a revival among players of all tribes.

HIDATSA DANCE SONG

HIDATSA

In 1804, the Lewis and Clark Expedition encountered the Hidatsa living in earthen lodges along the banks of the Missouri in what is now central North Dakota. The name "Hidatsa" is probably derived from the name of one of their larger villages at the time of this encounter. Lewis and Clark referred to the Hidatsa in their journals as "Minitari" while French-Canadian traders referred to them as "Gros Ventres des Missouri."

The Hidatsa, Mandan, and Arikira were closely allied and followed similar life-styles, practicing agriculture (growing squash, corn and beans in particular), supplemented by some hunting and trading. Of the three tribes, the Hidatsa ventured farthest to the west to fight traditional enemies. Their knowledge of routes to and through the Rocky Mountains provided Lewis and Clark with valuable information significantly contributing to the success of their mission.

A smallpox epidemic in 1837 nearly exterminated the Mandan and Hidatsa forcing survivors to consolidate villages and strengthen the intertribal alliance. In 1845, the remaining Hidatsa, Mandan and Arikira moved to the vicinity of Fort Berthold, North Dakota, where their descendents continue to reside. More can be learned of the life-style and culture of these groups from the Knife River Indian Village National Historical Site in North Dakota, and the Three Affiliated Tribes Museum in New Town, North Dakota.

I learned this flute version of a popular Hidatsa dance song from a Mandan-Hidatsa performer now living near Washington, DC.

CHAPTER **6**

A MYRIAD OF VOICES · GUIDED LISTENING EXPERIENCES

Photo on the previous page: The Drum at a gathering, Ft. Hall, Idaho: open-air recording studio complete with microphones and tape recorders large and small.
(Photo: John Running © 1992)

A MYRIAD OF VOICES

GUIDED LISTENING EXPERIENCES

ROOTED IN TRADITION

Limited only by imagination

The following six guided listening experiences are intended to reveal just a hint of the broad range of styles, structure, instrumentation and composition in use today by Native American musicians and composers, and also by others working with authentic Native American core materials. This brief introduction to the varied palette that includes Indian rock, works for symphonic band, traditional ceremonial music, New Age and jazz, will open your ears and mind to the limitless possibilities found in contemporary Native American music. Included are listings of the offerings of several recording companies that specialize in Native American performers. This is only the beginning—a world both ancient and futuristic awaits you.

The Porcupine Singers

"PICTURE SONG"
A LAKOTA RABBIT DANCE SONG

***Rabbit Dance Songs of the Lakota* by the Porcupine Singers**
Canyon Records [CR 6161-C] Lyrics, translation, and
recording © 1987, Canyon Records.
(Used by permission.)

"**P**icture Song" dates back to the 1940s and deals
with the universal theme of love, rejection, and "breaking up"
found in popular music throughout the world. The Porcupine
Singers are a popular Lakota group from South Dakota.
Recently, they gained a wide audience when they provided the
traditional Native American music for several scenes in the
award-winning motion picture *Dances With Wolves*.

FOCUS:
LANGUAGE AND FORM
1. Use of lyrics in a Native American language (Lakota, in
   this case)
2. Use of vocables
3. Form in Native American music

LAKOTA LYRICS:
Dearie waemaya Kiyaska
naweh unwe
Wanna hena la kte.
Itowapi ki micuna unsie.

ENGLISH TRANSLATION:
Dearie, I heard that you talked about me
Now it's going to be over.
Give my picture back
and don't come and see me any more.

LOCATE:

While looking at a map of the United States:
• Locate South Dakota and North Dakota.
• Locate major reservations for Lakota peoples including Pine Ridge, Standing Rock, Rosebud.

THE ROUND DANCE SONG FORM:

The traditional round dance song (social dance) of the Plains tribes may be divided into several distinct sections:

LEAD: An introduction normally sung by one person. Sung in vocables.

SECOND: A repeat of the lead sung by the entire group. Often, the second overlaps the lead by several notes. Sung in Vocables.

CHORUS: The main verse of the song sung by entire group. The chorus may be in vocables, an original Native American language, English, or any combination. The chorus of "Picture Song" is sung in Lakota (women's version) with the addition of the English word "Dearie" used as a term identifying the one to whom the song is addressed.

FIRST ENDING: A brief section often sung on a single pitch at the end of the chorus. Sung in vocables.

FINAL ENDING: A brief coda similar to other endings but with a drum cue indicating that this is the final ending.

Note: *Accented drum beats often serve as signals to the singers concerning repeats, endings, and changes in the song.*

LISTEN:

As you listen to the recording of Picture Song:
• Note the traditional round dance form and identify the component parts as they occur.
• Note the use of the Lakota language for text and differentiate between vocables and lexicals (words with particular meaning).
• Identify vocables used in the song.
• Find and identify "borrowed" English words used within the text.
• Do a rabbit or round dance to the music.

FOLLOW UP:

THE MUSIC OF THE PORCUPINE SINGERS
Listen to another recording and identify sections of the round dance form as they occur. Other recordings by this group are available from Canyon Records, including:
• CR 8006 *At Thunder Ring*
• CR 8007 *Traditional Sioux Songs*
• CR 8010 *At the University of South Dakota*
• CR 6192 *Rabbit Songs of the Lakota Vol. 2*

103

(Photo by Martha and Terry Hollinger)

Glafiro "Papos" Perez,
Deer Dancer

"CUERO MOHELAM"
A YAQUI PASCOLA DANCE

Yaqui Ritual and Festive Music
Canyon Records [CR 6140] ©1976; Side 2, Selection 1.
(Used by permission.)

Yaqui Deer Dance Rattle

The Yaqui (Yoeme) originally lived in the state of Sonora in northern Mexico. During the decades of civil unrest and revolution in Mexico during the early twentieth century, a number of Yaqui relocated in Arizona where several villages retain a strong Yaqui tradition. Upon first contact with Spanish missionaries during the colonial period, many Yaqui converted to the Catholic religion and adopted numerous Spanish customs, largely as a way of survival. Yaquis, however, combined elements of the new Catholic religion with traditional Yaqui beliefs to create a unique Yaqui religion. [Readers are referred to the writings of Edward Spicer for an in-depth study of Yaqui cultural history.] The Pascola is a ritual that blends Catholic holy week (Easter) rites with some of the traditional Yaqui spring time rituals encompassing rebirth and renewal. The Pascola dances often start off with European instruments and then progress to add Native American instruments and stylistic elements. The central figures include Deer Dancers, (see sidebar) and Pascola (Pahko'ola) dancers—ritual clowns who make fun of, hunt, tease and torment the deer. They wear special

A BALANCED LIFE

Glafiro "Papos" Perez is sixteen years old, and has been a Deer Dancer for six years. In his busy life in Old Pascua Yaqui Village in Tucson, Arizona he balances the demands of school, sports, friends, music, and poetry writing with what is closest to his heart and spirit: his Yoeme heritage. One of about twenty-seven Deer Dancers among the Yoeme, he is carrying on a tradition passed down in his family for generations. To prepare for a Deer Dance he puts on his great-great-great-grandfather's *reboso*, a special woven cloth; *rihhutiam, a* belt with deer hooves; ankle rattles made from giant Mexican moth cocoons filled with pebbles; and the head of a deer. He dances accompanied by singers who play rasps and a gourd water drum, *va kuvahe* that makes a sound like a deer's heartbeat. "Being part of the Deer Dance makes me proud to be a Yaqui. The Deer Dance stands for all the good in the world."
(Excerpted from "Glafiro: A Young Yoeme Deer Dancer" by Glafiro Perez and Emily Vance. (*Native Peoples*, Winter 1993. Used by permission.)

carved masks, and also function in the role of master of ceremonies.

Yaqui musicians incorporated elements of Spanish instruments such as the guitar and violin, creating ingenious homegrown instruments. These were played with the Mexican harp and existing Yaqui instruments, such as large gourd rattles, rasps placed against resonators, drums, and a three-hole whistle/flute. (The Yaqui violin is a square shape rather than having the curved, pinched waist of the European violin.)

Some Yaqui musics—mostly older ritual dances such as the Deer Dance—use only the traditional instruments. Newer songs and dances use a combination of traditional instruments with handcrafted versions of Spanish-style instruments. Melodies are a blend of traditional Yaqui music and European folk songs with texts in either Yaqui or Spanish. Many dances are also a blend of European folk dance steps with older Native American dances. Over the centuries, the musical styles have become so intermingled that it is no longer possible to accurately distinguish what was European in origin and what was taken from the original Yaqui styles. Some of the music bears a strong resemblance to the sound of Mexican mariachi ensembles.

Musicians on this recording are Marcos Zaviva Cochemea, Luis Jiocamea Cupisi, Conrrado Madrid Molina, Ignacio Pluma Blanca Aite, Fernando Contreras and Juan León Valencia.

FOCUS:
CROSS-CULTURAL INFLUENCES
1. Use of Native American instruments in Yaqui music.
2. Use of European-derived instruments in Yaqui music.
3. Blend of European and Native American styles: the process of cross-cultural influences in Yaqui music.

LOCATE:
While looking at a map of North America:
• Locate the southwestern United States and the state of Arizona.
• Locate the state of Sonora in northern Mexico.
• Locate major Yaqui settlements.

LOOK:
Show photos of Yaqui musicians, dancers, and instruments
• Note clothing, instrument particulars, and dance postures.

LISTEN:
While listening to the recording of "Cuero Mohelam":
• Identify Native American and European-derived instruments.
• Discuss the blending of Yaqui and Spanish cultures.

FOLLOW-UP:
• Read "Glafiro: A Young Yoeme Deer Dancer" in *Native Peoples* magazine, Winter 1993, pp. 46-50; play other selections from *Yaqui Ritual and Festive Music*; identify the instruments.

R. Carlos Nakai/Jackalope

LISTENING EXPERIENCE

3

"...THEN THERE WAS WOOD"
CONTEMPORARY FUSION

***Weavings,* performed by Jackalope.**
Canyon Records [CR 7002] © 1988.
(Used by permission.)

Jackalope is a contemporary Native American group consisting of R. Carlos Nakai, Larry Yanez, Richard Carbajal and Darrell Flint. R. Carlos Nakai, leader of Jackalope, is one of the best known Native American musicians active today. His numerous recordings include traditional music for the Native American flute, two albums by Jackalope, and "new age" music with several artists. His recording *Cycles* is used as the background music for the Heard Museum multi-media presentation "Our Voices, Our Land." Martha Graham choreographed five sections of *Cycles* as the ballet "Night Chant." He also has composed a number of television and film scores.

The music of Jackalope blends ethnic melodies, rhythms, and instruments with modern technologies and urban music styles to create what the group refers to as "SynthacousticpunkarachiNavajazz." Performances by Jackalope employ improvisation, music, dance, visual art, and storytelling and dramatic theatrical effects. Performers may add to the excitement by popping up from anywhere in the theater. Stories for these performances are drawn from North American, Aztec, and modern ethnic sources.

FOCUS:
CROSS-CULTURAL INFLUENCES IN CONTEMPORARY NATIVE AMERICAN MUSIC.

1. Elements of Native American music included in fusion music such as this:
   (a) use of Native American instruments;
   (b) incorporation of sounds of animals and nature;
   (c) use of Native American melodic themes.
2. Elements of jazz, rock, and urban musical styles such as:
   (a) use of synthesizer, guitar, bass guitar;
   (b) use of typical jazz-rock rhythmic backgrounds;
   (c) improvisation in jazz-rock style.

LISTEN:

While listening to the recording of "Then there was Wood":
- Identify Native American instruments (Native American flute, shell trumpet, whistles, gamecalls, rattles, and drums).
- Identify jazz-rock instruments (guitar, Synthesizer, drum set), sounds of animals and nature, Native American melodic motifs and jazz-rock improvisational melodies.

FOLLOW-UP:
THE MUSIC OF R. CARLOS NAKAI:

Among Nakai's numerous recordings are:

On the Canyon Label (address in appendix):
- CR 609 *Emergence*; CR 610 *Canyon Triology*;
- CR 612 *Earth Spirit*; CR 613 *Journeys*; CR 614 *Cycles*;
- CR 615 *Changes*; CR 7001 *Jackalope*;
- CR 7002 *Jackalope-Weavings*; CR 7006 *Carry the Gift*;
- CR 7007 *Winter Dreams*; CR 7010 *Ancestral Voices,*
- CR 7014 *Spirit Horses*

Albums on labels other than Canyon Records but available through Canyon or music stores include:
Natives; *Sundance Season*; *Desert Dance* and *Migration*.

Pueblo Village at Laguna

"SUNRISE CALL"
A VOICE LIFTED TO THE NEW DAY

Music from Zuni Pueblo **by Chester Mahooty and Family**
Tribal Music International [TMI 008] © 1990.
(Used by permission.)

Sunrise songs are performed at dawn to thank the sun for returning with its guarantee that life will continue to exist for another day. Many agriculturally-based cultures had similar rites to seek continued fertility and prosperity. Among another southwestern group, there is a proverb that to be successful and live a happy life, one must rise early each day and greet the sun. The Hopi present newborn children to the sun on a specific day after birth.

Chester Mahooty is a well-known and respected Zuni singer and composer. (He is also a master jewelry-maker.) He performs with the Zuni Rainbow Dancers (founded by his mother-in-law and led by his wife Dorothy) and the American Indian Dance Theatre. As a member of these groups, Mahooty has toured North America and Europe and has appeared on television in a taped performance by the American Indian Dance Theatre.

Members of the performing group on this recording are: Chester Mahooty—vocals and drum; Dorothy Mahooty—gourd shakers, bells, vocals; Brenner Mahooty (their grandson)—shaker. All members of the Zuni Rainbow Dancers are related by blood and/or clan.

108

FOCUS:

STYLE AND SUBSTANCE:

1. Recognize vocal style traits, musical texture and timbre from Southwest Native American culture.
2. Gain an understanding of Zuni culture and history through a brief overview.
3. Compare and contrast vocal and instrumental versions of the same song.

LOCATE:

While looking at a map of the southwestern United States:
• Locate New Mexico and Zuni Pueblo

While listening to the taped renditions of "Sunrise Call":
• Discuss Southwestern Native American vocal style (see Chapter One).
• Discuss Southwestern Native American flute style (see Chapter Four).

LISTEN:

• Compare the instrumental version and vocal versions.
• Refer to this listening guide as an aid.
  - Vocal *or* Instrumental
  - Accompanied *or* Unaccompanied
  - Same rhythms *or* Differing rhythms (in each version / between versions)
  - Describe melody of vocal version.
  - Describe melody of instrumental version.

FOLLOW-UP:

THE AMERICAN INDIAN DANCE THEATER

This large troupe of dancers and musicians tours actively throughout the United States, performing a great variety of dances from all culture areas. *Finding the Circle*, the video of their television concert aired on public television's *Great Performances* program is an excellent introduction to many dances as well as vocal and instrumental music. The voice-over narration by members of the group creates a deeper understanding of the importance of the traditional music and dances in maintaining the Native American heritage.

Far West Photography

XIT

LISTENING EXPERIENCE
5

"NIHAA SHIL HOZHO" (I AM HAPPY ABOUT YOU)
XIT: THE SOUND OF AMERICAN INDIAN ROCK

Plight of the Redman **performed by XIT.**
Sounds of America Records SOAR [101-CD].
Lyrics, translation, and recording © 1989,
(Used by permission.)

Musical taste and style are as diverse among Native Americans as among the remainder of American society. There are New Age, country-western, gospel and rock groups that have been formed by musicians from all tribal backgrounds. They find an enthusiastic audience in the cities as well as on the reservation lands—listeners who will request their favorites on the local radio stations, and purchase them at the nearest store.

Many of these styles were brought to the native communities and reservations through radio broadcasts and also by students and workers returning to their communities after living and working in white society. Native musicians copied these styles and added unique "Indian" flavors to the stew. A. Paul Ortega, for example, created a syncretic style combining country-blues guitar with traditional Apache songs. Sharon Burch performs in a folk-rock style reminiscent of Joan Baez using lyrics in her native Navajo. Buffy Saint-Marie has long blended topical and spiritual themes in her songs, sung in a penetrating, distinctive

110

vibrato. Since the 1960s Buffy Saint-Marie has been able to speak to the hearts and minds of her people while reaching the non-Indian folk and folk-pop audience with her strong message and equally strong presence and appearance.

R. Carlos Nakai performs traditional flute, jazz, and New Age styles.

Perhaps the most successful Native American rock group is XIT. XIT performs a creative blend of rock and traditional styles. Lyrics often include vocables and various Native languages in addition to English with topics drawn from the Native American tradition. The drum set used by the group is an ingenious mix of Native American drums with cymbals and rock accessories while electric guitars, acoustic guitars, and keyboards combine with Native American rattles, bells, and natural sounds to create a unique style which remains distinctly Native American. The group takes full advantage of the range of studio techniques, equipment and influences available to the contemporary popular performer.

Included on this selection are Michael Martin, Mac Suazo, Lee Herrera, R.C. Gariss, Jr., and Tom Bee. Members of the group come from a diverse tribal background. The name XIT is an acronym for "Crossing of Indian Tribes" to represent this multiple identity. The group consciously avoided use of a stereotypical name such as "Yellowhorse," "Warriors," etc. XIT's awareness of Native issues and consciousness is reflected in many of their songs such as "The Coming of the White Man," "I Was Raised (in Indian Ways)," and "War Cry."

XIT continues to perform and records for Sounds of America Records. Other albums by XIT include: *Silent Warrior, Entrance, Backtrackin', Relocation,* and *Drums Across the Atlantic.* Composer/lyricist Tom Bee (of Dakota descent) has also released a solo album, *Color Me Red.* (XIT International Fan Club, PO Box 8207, Albuquerque, NM 87198 USA.)

FOCUS:
LANGUAGE AND FORM:
1. Use of lyrics in a Native American language and English (Navajo and English)
2. Use of vocables
3. Form in Native American music.

LYRICS:
Composer/lyricist Tom Bee has said that the English lyrics should be considered as a poetic rendering of the Navajo verse. It is difficult to translate Navajo literally into English and still preserve the subtleties. (The Navajo words are transcribed phonetically here.) The lyrics below are copyrighted (1989) and are used with the permission of Tom Bee.

"Nihaa Shil Hozho"

Yinilye hozho
nihaa shil hozho hey ya al ah
Taa aniidla
Oh lah.

Yinilye hozho
heh tah aniid heh yah ateed
Taa aniidla
Oh lah.

I call you sunflower
You're the flower that happiness grows:
the beauty of your smile and the warmth of
your eyes
bring sunshine into my soul.

Yinilye hozho
nihaa shil hozho hey yah al ah
Taa aniidla
Oh lah.

Living, Loving
I am happy about you
together forever
My young maiden.
I speak the truth.

Don't be afraid, don't be afraid.

LISTEN:
1. Identify the contemporary instruments in the selection,
   including electric and acoustic slide and rhythm guitars,
   drums and bass, violin/synth.
2. Identify the traditional instruments: drums, bells, rattle.
   (The drum set includes traditional log drums of various
   sizes.)
3. Compare contemporary mainstream rock music to the
   style, instruments and intended audience in Native
   American rock music.

FOLLOW UP:
Another group that is very popular is Southern Scratch, a
five-piece band that specializes in "chicken scratch" a cousin
of polka and norteño (US-Mexican border music). This lively
music, called *waila* by the Tohono O'odham who are the
main practitioners of the sound, features guitar, saxophone,
accordion, and drums, with maracas and cowbells on the
side. Canyon Records has released two albums by the band.

Tatanka-Ptecila (Short Bull)

LISTENING EXPERIENCE

6

GHOST DANCE
A WORK FOR SYMPHONIC BAND

Augustana College Concert Band (premier recording)
Dr. Bruce T. Ammann conducting, February 3, 1993,
John F. Kennedy Center for the Performing Arts,
Washington D.C.
(Provided courtesy of the composer, Dr. Quincy Hilliard.)

Contemporary composers no longer are satisfied with producing the hackneyed, pseudo-Indian music so common in preceding decades (the Boom-boom-boom-boom movie scores, for instance). Culturally aware composers now seek authenticity in sound and appropriateness of use when composing works dealing with Native American topics for motion picture and television scores, educational band literature, and symphonic works. William Hill used source material from Natalie Curtis' *The Indian's Book* as the basis for his *Sioux Variants*. James Ployhar adapted Native American melodies in easy band settings, and James Curnow successfully captured the spirit of Native American music in his *Legend and Sundance*. Louis Ballard, prominent Native American musician and educator has produced numerous works for various media using more authentic materials and instruments as well.

Representative of this trend in authentically representing the sounds of Native America in symphonic music is Quincy Hilliard's recent symphonic suite, *Ghost Dance*. After accepting a commission from Augustana College in Sioux Falls, South Dakota, to write a major band work commemorating the Wounded Knee Massacre (December 29, 1890), Dr. Hilliard sought advice from authorities on Native American culture, studied recordings of authentic music, learned performance techniques of Native American instruments which could be adapted for band, and sought counsel from Native American spiritual leaders regarding how the music should be incorporated appropriately into a traditionally non-Indian musical form. The work was intended to be a musical offering in the spirit of reconciliation between Indian and non-Indian people. (In 1990, Governor George Mickelson of South Dakota declared a Year of Reconciliation, to be followed by a Century of Reconciliation in South Dakota.)

Sounds representing Native American eagle bone whistles, and authentic flutes, drums and rattles were added to the traditional wind ensemble to give a new musical flavor. A Ghost Dance song, "Wanagi Wacipi Olowan," by Tatanka-Ptecila (Short Bull), a prominent leader in the Dakota ghost dance movement of the 1880s and 1890s, serves as the thematic basis for parts of two movements of the work. Prefacing each movement are statements by Native American leaders setting the mood for the programmatic content. Finally, the sounds of a crying baby—representing Lost Bird, a child who survived the battle—add emotional impact to this highly charged and sensitive work. The result is a musical offering in the spirit of reconciliation between Indian and non-Indian peoples.

Movement I sets the mood of the *hanblecca* (vision quest) using chanting and fragments of the Ghost Dance song. Movement II evokes the hope and comfort atmosphere of the Ghost Dance with significant sections of Short Bull's musical material easily recognizable during the second theme. Movement III depicts the horrifying slaughter of women, children, and old men by troops of the Seventh Cavalry on the morning of December 29, 1890. The final measures portray throwing frozen bodies into a mass grave at the place called Wounded Knee.

A complete performance of Movement II and brief excerpts from Movements I and III are presented here. Listen for the use of Native American instruments throughout the work and notice phrases based upon "Wanagi Wacipi Olowan," presented on the next page as sung by Short Bull to Natalie Curtis, and found with additional cultural and historical background in *The Indians' Book*, pages 41-48.

I. INCANTATION:

"Hear me, Grandfather, so the people may live."
- Martin Brokenleg, Rosebud Sioux, Professor of Minority Studies at Augustana College

II. DANCE OF THE GHOSTS:

"All Indians must dance, everywhere, keep on dancing. Pretty soon in next spring Great Spirit come."
(Wovoka, Paiute Messiah)

III. THE MASSACRE:

"There was no hope on earth, and God seemed to have forgotten us."
(Chief Red Cloud)

WANAGI WACIPI OLOWAN
(Ghost or Spirit Dance Songs)

Unlike many songs which come to individuals in visions who then retain ownership of the songs, the Ghost Dance songs, although learned in visions during dancing, were given freely to all participants of the movement.

THE GHOST DANCE RELIGION

Wovoka, a Paiute prophet known as the Father, inspired the Ghost Dance in the late 1880s. The Plains peoples had experienced drastic changes in their lives as a result of their encounter with Europeans, and many were in despair, sick, starving and abused, confined to reservations, denied their traditional lifeways. Wovoka's message was of peace, an end to fighting and illness, and a return of the dead from the spirit-world. A holy circle dance and its many songs (given through trance-visions) was a critical part of the peaceful movement, which spread rapidly across the Plains. Groups met and danced, sharing their vision for a better world. Many whites found the movement threatening.

Soldiers were called in to stop the dancing at the Pine Ridge Reservation. A single warning shot from a Dakota rifle was answered by a storm of machine gun fire from the troops, resulting in the violent death of nearly three hundred men, women and children at Wounded Knee. Their frozen bodies were thrown into an open trench. The Ghost Dance Religion in its original form perished and was buried there as well.

I. Ateyapi kin
Maka owancaya
Lowan nisipe-lo
Heya-po (2x)
Oyakapo—he!(2x)
(English: Thus the Father said,
Lo, he now commands
All on earth to sing, to sing now.
Thus he has spoken,
Tell afar his message!)

II. Ina, hekuye, (2x)
Misunkala ceya-ya omani, (2x)
Ina, hekuye (2x)
Ate heye-lo (2x)
(English: Mother, oh come back,
Little brother calls as he seeks thee, weeping,
Mother, oh, come back,
Says the Father.)

III. He, he wanna wawate, (2x)
Wasna watinkte (2x)
(English: He, he joyous feast we now,
Eating pemmican!)

The reference to pemmican, spiced and pounded dried buffalo meat, relates in part to a prophecy of a time when whites would be taken back across the ocean, and the buffalo and its many gifts would return.

Dr. Quincy Hilliard is Assistant Professor of Theory and Composition at the University of Southwestern Louisiana, Lafayette, Louisiana. *Ghost Dance* is available in manuscript from the composer.

CHAPTER **7**

MAKING INSTRUMENTS THE NEW OLD-FASHIONED WAY

Photo on the previous page: Carved wooden drums of various sizes and decoration at Santa Clara Pueblo, New Mexico. This type is a closed drum: skin covers both top and bottom.
 (Photo: John Running © 1992)

MAKING INSTRUMENTS

THE NEW OLD-FASHIONED WAY

Making Native American instruments for classroom use should not prove a daunting task to anyone. Designs are simple, construction logical. "Standards" are those of folk art, not those of slick mass-production culture, which is not to say the results are slipshod, only that they will not be cookie-cutter duplications. Tremendous leeway is allowed in creative design and decoration. Basically, if it makes the intended sound, it is correct.

Anyone who has attended a pow-wow or cultural fair has already become aware of the ingenuity of Native American in creating instruments from virtually any material. Traditional bone rattles and gourd rattles are still preferred by traditional Native Americans, however, new materials and designs gain acceptance quite readily. For example, a popular rattle is simply a metal (aluminum) salt shaker attached to a stick (dowel rod) and decorated with feathers; fiberglass bicycle flag poles are used for more flexible and long-lasting drum beaters; Copenhagen snuff can lids are now the preferred source of tin which is cut and rolled in the process of making dance jingles.

Because of their deep respect for Mother Earth, Native Americans have long been environmentalists (even before the term was created) and construct instruments as well as other cultural objects from "recycled" materials. Projects making instruments from such materials would be a good starting point for a teacher wishing to integrate music with social issues such as environmental concerns.

I learned how to make each of the instruments described in this section the old- fashioned way—from Native Americans who were themselves making instruments. An elderly Yaqui gentlemen gave a rattle-making lesson in the shade of a brush arbor in a small community near Phoenix; an Apache woman allowed me to watch and "help" make dance jingles; the owner of a trading post whiled away a customer-less afternoon showing how to make the drum beaters and drum rattles. There were no "by-the-numbers" instructions to follow in any of the situations—I learned to make the instruments by copying each step of the process taken by the person "teaching." This approach should be the most effective (and least intimidating) technique for guiding others to construct their own instruments. Patience and nurturing are the key ingredients to a successful outcome.

I wrote the instructions based upon the experience of learning to make the instruments by rote— "see what I do, do as I do"—methodology.

Substitution of readily obtainable materials for natural materials has been made in several cases. For example, art clay has been substituted for the natural mixture of clay and sand used in firming the end of a gourd rattle, and white craft glue has been substituted in many instances for the hide glue made and used by most Native American craftsmen. If you have access to the real thing, so much the better.

So...gather materials, roll up your sleeves, and start making instruments to use when your group performs the songs and dances from this collection.

DANCE JINGLES

Many Native American tribes attached bits of shell, stone, and metal to dance clothing to create a jingling sound when the dancer moved. Following the establishment of trading posts, dancers began to use bits of tin cut from tobacco containers and tin cans obtained from the traders because of the clearer sound of the metal jingles. The Ojibway say that jingle dances originated during a time of pestilence when many people were dying. The medicine person had a dream: if the community would make jingles and dance the Creator would heal the village. The medicine person fulfilled the vow made during a vision quest, to hold this dance, and the entire village was healed of the illness.

Contemporary dancers prefer the lids from Copenhagen snuff cans as the materials for jingle-style dance bells. These may be purchased from Native American suppliers either as finished jingles or in their original shape. Some dancers observed at pow-wows are also using the tops of microwave soup containers with leather strips attached to the pull tabs. Sometimes large harness bells are attached to belts or part of the clothing to enhance the sound of the jingle-style dance bells.

By using the materials and instructions below, dance bells similar to those used by contemporary jingle dancers may be constructed for use in the classroom. The process of making "traditional" jingles, cut from bits of tin or aluminum, is not recommended for younger children due to the possibility of injury from handling sharp edges. The "contemporary" jingle, rolled from tobacco or snuff can lids, is safer and equally authentic. Some dancers affix a certain number of jingles for each year of dancing, so that the longer one has been a jingle dancer, the more jingles will be attached to the regalia.

TRADITIONAL DESIGN:

MATERIALS:
- Tin or aluminum cans
- Strips of rawhide or leather lacing

TOOLS:
- Tin snips
- Needle nose pliers
- Sewing supplies—needles, thread, etc.

Figure 1

PROCEDURE:

1. Flatten cans and cut bits of metal in the shape and dimensions shown in Figure 1.
Caution: edges of the metal are sharp and care must be taken to avoid injury.

2. Tie a knot in one end of a 4" strip of rawhide or leather lacing; center lacing on piece of tin as shown above.

3. Using pliers, bend metal piece around lacing in elongated bell shape as shown above.

4. Jingles may now be attached to fabric or leather for use as necklaces.

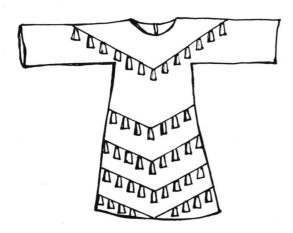 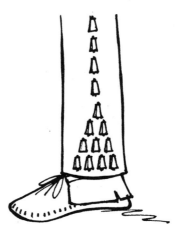

5. Or they may be sewn onto a dance dress, skirt and separate top or shirt, or used in designs on the trousers of male dancers.

CONTEMPORARY DESIGN

MATERIALS:

• "Tobacco lids" (although these were originally lids from snuff cans, these lids are now frequently manufactured specifically for use in making dance jingles making purchase of tobacco products or searching for discarded lids unnecessary). Lids are usually sold in bags of 100 and are available from virtually any Native American craft supplier for approximately $12 per 100.

• Bias tape (available from any fabric store).

TOOLS:

• Jingle roller (both wooden and metal rolling sticks are available the difference being simply durability—the wooden roller will last for about 300 jingles while the metal roller has an almost infinite lifetime). Current prices for rollers are: wooden = $5; metal = $15

• Needle-nose pliers

• Fabric scissors

PROCEDURE:

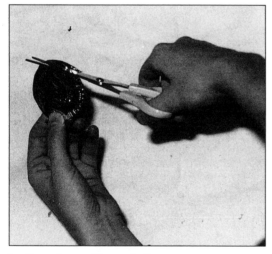

1. Cut edges off carefully, then cut straight across one edge of the circle.

2. Smooth the edges and place the straight section into the slot in the jingle roller.

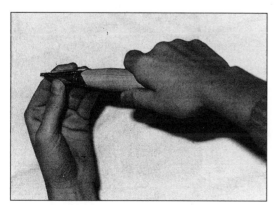

3. Roll lid around rolling stick until desired cone shape is achieved.

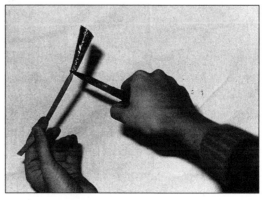

4. Place ribbon through cone, crimp end of jingle with pliers; attach to clothing.

WRIST/ANKLE BELLS

Bands of bells are often added to regalia by Native American dancers. These bands may be sewn to the clothing or strapped around ankles, wrists, upper arms, etc. As noted above, bits of shell may be used for decoration and for sound. Small round "advertising" mirrors were also popular decorations on old dance regalia, now available in bulk from craft suppliers.

Use the materials and instructions below to construct basic bands of bells that are ready for further creative decorating.

MATERIALS:
- Small "Christmas" bells (larger bells may also be used as noted previously)
- Leather or fabric strips approximately two inches by six inches
- Leather lacing

TOOLS:
- Mat knife.

PROCEDURE:
1. Make single slits at ends of leather with mat knife. Then, make evenly spaced slits in groups of two as shown below:

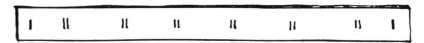

2. Weave leather lacing through slits, attaching bells to leather strap:

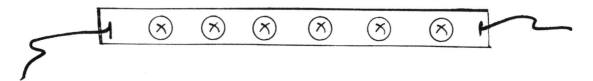

OPTIONAL:
Decorate bands by drawing Native American Designs on leather and/or gluing dyed feathers under bells.

A SIMPLER OPTION:
Substitute strips of wide elastic for leather straps and mark intervals at which bells are to be attached. Then, sew bells onto elastic and sew elastic together to form band. This will not have as authentic an appearance, but will provide easy-to-use wrist/ankle bands possibly more suitable for use with younger children.

"RECYCLED" RATTLE

Rattles are an integral part of any Native American music. By using the materials and instructions below, a simple Native American-style rattle may be constructed for classroom use.

Native Americans have deep respect for the environment. The use of recyclable materials in constructing this rattle can be used as an opening for discussion of (a) environmental awareness, (b) Native American culture—particularly as related to nature, (c) other ways in which materials may be recycled for classroom use. Any size of container may be used, as rattle sizes did vary among tribes. Ray Sark, descendant of the hereditary chiefs of the Lennox Island Band of the Micmac tribe (Prince Edward Island, Canada) said that tin vegetable cans were frequently used after the mid-Nineteenth Century because they made "louder" rattles. Materials were readily available and traditional construction methods were simple to adapt.

MATERIALS:

• Plastic, metal, or cardboard container. (These instructions will specifically use a plastic container, with a plastic snap-on lid which may be found in any supermarket powdered drink mix section. Adapt the instructions for other types of containers.)
• Stick or dowel rod approximately 10" to 12" in length.
• Nail (broad, flat head).
• Brown paper grocery sacks or construction paper.
• Pebbles, beans, unpopped popcorn (a great use for unpopped kernels) or other objects to create rattling inside container.
• "Super-glue"
• White liquid glue.
• Optional: wooden craft beads, yarn, dyed feathers, fabric (leather, chamois, or felt), leather lacing.

TOOLS:

• Hammer
• Mat knife
• Scissors

PROCEDURE:

1. Remove plastic lid, mark size of stick (rod) in center, cut out opening for stick with mat knife:

2. Place stick (dowel rod) into container and nail to center of container bottom as shown below:

3. Place pebbles or other rattling objects into container.

4. Push container lid down stick handle almost to container. Then place drops of a "super glue" product at several points on lid rim. Snap lid onto container and hold approximately 45 seconds to set.

5. Cut strips of grocery bag (or construction paper) to size of container and paste around container. Decorate with Native American motifs.

OPTIONAL:

Finish the rattle with typical embellishments:

1. Tie or glue natural or dyed feathers to strips of leather lacing or yarn and tie through small wooden craft bead. When attaching stick to container, simply place the bead between the top of the container and the nail, then hammer firmly as shown below:

2. Cut circles of fabric (or leather or chamois) and place on top and bottom of completed rattle. Use leather-needle to thread lacing or rawhide strips as shown below:

GOURD RATTLE

Native American rattles may be made from virtually any available materials (vegetable cans, rawhide, salt shakers, etc.), but the type of rattle most associated with Native American music is a simple dried gourd rattle. These rattles may be of any size or shape and have as much or as little decoration as desired. ("Natural" gourd rattles are as authentic as brightly painted and decorated rattles—the final product is left to the imagination of the maker.)

MATERIALS:
- Dried gourd of desired size and shape
- Rattles—may be seeds from gourd, pebbles, other seeds, beans, unpopped popcorn duds
- Twine, heavy string, or yarn
- White glue
- Stick of appropriate size (dowel rod is OK)
- Optional: paints for decorations
- Optional: plasticine clay to reinforce neck of rattle
- Optional: feathers, beads or other materials for decoration

TOOLS:
- Sharp knife or saw
- Spoon, knife, or other scraping tool
- Paint brushes for decorations

PROCEDURE:
1. Cut off narrow end of gourd with knife or saw:

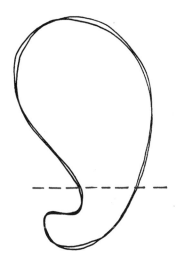

2. Remove seeds and membrane from inside gourd with spoon or knife—this is very important, as too much membrane remaining in the gourd may cause rotting, or uneven drying resulting in cracking, withering, or shrinking.

3. Dry gourd thoroughly—this may be done naturally by placing in warm, dry location for up to two weeks (until gourd is uniformly dried and hardened) or by placing in a low temperature oven (150°-ish) for as long as necessary. Check the gourd frequently during drying to determine if more scraping is needed to remove dried membrane and seeds (assuring more even drying and maintaining shape). It is during this step that most problems and failures occur.

4. When gourd is dried, place rattle material inside the gourd. As you add the rattles, test the sound frequently to determine the correct amount for the sound you desire.

5. Put glue on end of stick (handle) and push handle inside gourd until the glued end touches the shell. If necessary, mold a reinforcing layer of clay around the handle to tightly seal the opening in the gourd.

6. Dip twine/string/yarn in white glue and wrap around base of handle and up the gourd to completely cover the opening and any reinforcing clay:

7. Decorate the gourd with Native-American inspired designs, if desired. Spray a coating of clear epoxy finish on gourd to preserve finish.

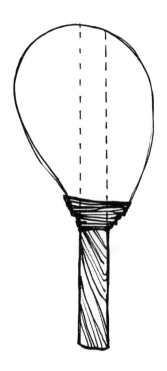

DRUM BEATERS

The design of drum beaters differs from tribe to tribe among the Native Americans. In addition, special designs may be used for specific types of music or to play specific types of drums. Three types of beaters will be described here and instructions given for their construction: Apache, Navajo drum rattle, and a "generic" beater in the style of the beater used by many tribes.

APACHE STYLE

MATERIALS:
- Fresh, thin branch approximately 15" to 18" in length. This branch should be strong, yet limber.
- Leather shoelaces or heavy wool yarn.

TOOLS:
- Sharp woodcarving knife.

PROCEDURE:
1. Bend branch to make a loop approximately 4" in diameter. It may be necessary to whittle at the bending point in order for the branch to make this loop.

2. Tie branch to hold in place.

Rawhide, Twine or
Yarn Lacing

End may need to be tapered for snug fit. Whittle to shape.

NAVAJO DRUMBEATER/RATTLE:

This instrument builds on the design of the Apache beater above creating a beater which adds the sound of rattling to the music. As we have seen in previous chapters, the Apache and Navajo are closely related tribes and have many cultural similarities.

MATERIALS: [In addition to those listed above for Apache Beater—]
- Cotton or wool fabric (Navajo prefer rawhide, if available)
- White glue
- Beans or pebbles
- Waxed paper

TOOLS:
- Sharp woodcarving knife
- Two small dessert or fruit bowls approximately 4" in diameter

PROCEDURE: After completion of Apache style beater--
1. Cut fabric in circular shape approximately 1-1/2" to 2 " larger than loop in beater.

2. Soak fabric in solution consisting of 3 parts white glue and 1 part water.

3. Place waxed paper in bowls (to prevent fabric from sticking to bowl) and lay fabric in bowl. When fabric dries, it should retain the shape of the bowl.

4. Put one piece of fabric on each side of loop and trim to 1/2" greater in diameter than the loop.

5. Cut holes around circle approximately 1/2" apart.

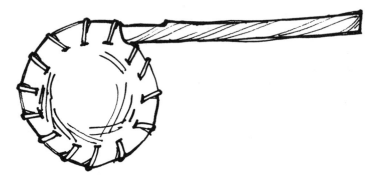

6. Lace yarn or lacing through holes. When lacing is about halfway complete, insert"rattles"(beans or whatever) inside fabric. Complete lacing.

Top view

GENERIC, ALL-PURPOSE DRUM BEATER

Many Native American musicians use a simple drum beater consisting of a stick with a padded head. The size of the beater is determined by the size of drum to be played. If there will be several drummers, the stick should be longer so the musicians are not overcrowded.

MATERIALS:
- Straight branch, dowel rod, or fiberglass bicycle flag holder cut to desired length.
- Fabric or rawhide material (chamois skin or a facsimile from an auto supply house is currently popular).
- Padding--wool, cotton, foam rubber.
- Leather lacing, needle and thread, skinny thong.

TOOLS:
- Scissors
- Woodcarving knife

PROCEDURE:

1. Cut stick for shaft of beater to desired length. If using fiberglass, *be careful*—splinters take a long time to work out of the skin!!

2. Cut the Fabric:
    - Option A: Cut an appropriately-sized circle or square of the chosen fabric. Cut holes for lacing around edge of material at 1/2" intervals.
    - Option B: Cut circle or square but do not cut holes in fabric.
    - Option C: Cut two identical lightbulb-shaped pieces of fabric; stitch seams.

3. Place padding material around tip of shaft; glue padding to shaft for greater security.

4. Add cover and secure:
- Using fabric from Option A:
Tightly lace cover around padding, weaving the lacing through the holes and tying tightly.
- Using fabric from Option B:
Spread cover over padding, secure with rubber band; conceal rubber band by wrapping leather lacing over it. Knot, and cut ends fairly short.
- Using stitched fabric from Option C:
Pull cover over padding, secure by winding thread or skinny thong around bottom edge.

OPTIONAL:
- Drill hole in end of shaft, pull thong through and tie into loose loop.

RASPS

Rasps are used by many Native American groups in traditional and contemporary popular music. These rasps are distinguished primarily by size.

The Yaqui, Tarahumara, and other desert peoples of southern Arizona and northern Mexico prefer a scraped rasp (morache) of a small diameter which produces as crisp high sound similar to that of a guiro. The rasp is placed with the end against an overturned bowl, basket, or gourd and played by scraping a smaller stick or a bone such as a sheep shoulder blade, used by the Hopi, across notches cut into the rasp. This sound may be heard in the traditional tribal music such as deer dances and the matichine dances which blend traditional Native American styles with those of European folk music. (See Listening Experience # 2.)

YAQUI-STYLE RASP:

A rasp similar to that used by the Yaqui people may be constructed by following these brief instructions:

MATERIALS:
- Straight branch or dowel approximately 1/2" to 3/4" in diameter and 18"-24" in length.
- Straight branch or dowel 1/4" in diameter and 10" in length.

TOOLS:
- Coping saw;
- Round file or sandpaper.

PROCEDURE:

1. Mark the larger dowel at 1/2" intervals leaving perhaps 6" for a handle on one end (another 2" may be left at the opposite end for a carved bird or animal head).

2. At every other mark, cut a "v" shape 1/4" deep.

3. File or sand rough edges in notches

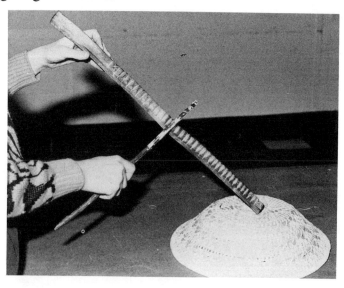

BEAR DANCE STYLE RASP:

Ute, Sioux, and other tribes using a rasp in their bear dances use a larger rasp to produce a loud, growling sound. This "bear rasp" is played by placing one end against an inverted washtub, a drum, or piece of sheet metal covering a hole in the ground. Obviously, the larger the resonator, the larger the sound. The rasp itself is often made from large sections of lumber to further enhance the volume.

The rasp may be played in a rhythmic tempo to accompany the social dances associated with the Bear Dance ritual or a player may improvise bear-like growls to accompany a solo dance in which the dancer mimics the bear, matching the sounds created by the rasp player.

A rasp similar to the one used in a bear dance may be constructed by following these instructions.

MATERIALS:
- Branch or dowel approximately 1 1/2" - 2" in diameter and 18" long
- Smaller branch or dowel approximately 1" in diameter and 10" long

TOOLS:
- Coping saw
- Round file or sandpaper

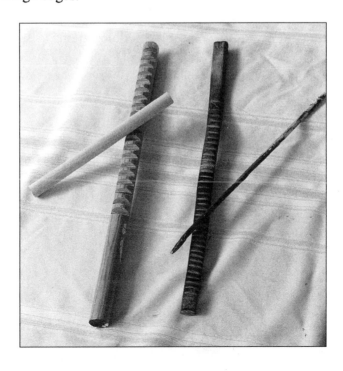

PROCEDURE:
1. Mark the larger dowel at 3/8" intervals leaving 6" to 8" at one end for a handle.

2. At every other mark, cut a "v" approximately 3/8" deep, making a straight cut down the center of the interval with 45-degree cuts made to meet the center cut.

3. File or sand the rough edges.

DRUMS

"Drum making cannot be rushed. Done correctly, it takes time." - Cochiti Drum Maker

Although Native American musicians are becoming quite creative in using various materials for rattles, drum beaters, etc., most still prefer to use a drum made of traditional materials by a master drum maker or make their own drums using traditional materials and methods. Perhaps this is because of the strong spiritual associations of the drum—the heartbeat of Mother Earth. Reasonably priced Native American drums are available from regional drum makers (see Appendix) or from Native American companies such as the Taos Drum Company that supplies many of the music stores and mail order catalogs specializing in authentic ethnic instruments. (If you are interested in purchasing an authentic drum from an educational supply company, take care to inquire about the manufacturer so that you do not find yourself with one stamped "Made in Taiwan"!)

Souvenir shops near reservations sometimes cater to the wishes of tourists seeking "cheap" Indian drums by selling plastic drums with a rubber drum head. These are usually found on the same rack as the rubber tomahawks and plastic spears. One Native American working in such a shop termed these items as "the Indian's revenge": "Imagine the misery of being cooped up all the way home from vacation in a car full of children banging those drums and trying to scalp their brothers and sisters!" he commented, only slightly tongue-in-cheek.

Many educational publications provide instructions for making "Indian" drums from coffee cans, oatmeal boxes, and other materials. Although these might produce passable noises for drum rhythms, do not refer to such items as Native American drums—they are a craft project only. Furthermore, the idea of providing every participant with a drum for playing "Indian" music is not consistent with Native American performance practice, where typically several players will be grouped on one large drum, or a select small group of drummers will each play a drum.

A fine discussion of drum making and the master drum maker/musician's philosophy may be found in Kate McGraw's "Where Drums are Born" in Indians of New Mexico. The methods of several master drum makers from Cochiti Pueblo are described. (For a fuller discussion of drums in *Moving Within the Circle*, turn to Chapter 2: "Voices of the Circle: Instruments.")

LOG DRUMS:

The following procedure is typical of the methods used in the Southwest for making log drums.

1. Cut cross section of log (preferably aspen or cottonwood), to desired length for drum, preferably using a tree that has fallen naturally.

2. Let log sections dry naturally until core is soft and flaky (sometimes as long as one year) then strip off bark.

3. Clear out the center core with a mallet and chisel; start at the center; let the section dry further between workings so the finished drum will not warp.

4. Sand and file both inside and outside of drum shell.

5. Cut drum heads to size from properly prepared, soaked cowhide. The process for preparing hide is lengthy and needs expert guidance. Purchasing rawhide from a supplier and soaking it for two to three days is an alternative.

6. Lace heads onto drum shell with rawhide lacing.

7. Dry several days away from uneven heat (e.g. wood stove) or hot spots (e.g. in direct sunlight).

8. Decorate as desired. Master drum makers usually leave drums unfinished if they are to be used by professional Native American musicians, who prefer to decorate their own drums. It is more common to find already-decorated drums being sold to the "tourist" or educational market.

WATER DRUM:

SOUTHWEST

The water drum of the Southwest is often a pottery jar or pot with a pronounced "lip." The jar is filled with "a couple of mouthfuls" of water, a hide head is soaked and stretched across the top of the jar, and a leather thong is tightly tied around the jar under the lip, to hold the head in place. After the head begins to dry, the drum is ready for playing. Some players use a chamois cloth for the head and a large rubber band (borrowed from their wife's aerobics class?) to hold the head in place.

NORTHEAST

Among tribes of the Northeast, wooden water drums are more common. These may be carved from a log as with Southwestern drums, but a bottom is left and a "bung hole" (closed with a stick, cork or stopper) is placed in the side for draining water. The process of making the water drum may also be similar to making a small barrel or keg. Indeed, some makers will utilize nail kegs, wine casks or other small pre-manufactured kegs for basic material. The head is held in place by either a wooden hoop specially carved to size or a leather thong. The piece of material used for the head extends loosely below the hoop, while being stretched tightly above it.

HAND DRUMS:

Single or double headed hand drums (or frame drums) may be made following the instructions for the log drum, beginning with a piece of log that is substantially a thin slice. Some makers will drill small holes in the side of the drum and lace leather through the holes. Others might tie laces together in the back so that the thongs may be squeezed to produce changes in pitch. Others will attach a handle. These are common among all tribes.

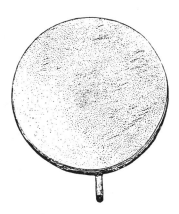

WHO, WHAT, WHEN, WHERE
APPENDIX

ODDS AND ENDS
• Where to Write for
Information
• Visiting a Reservation
• Chief Seattle's Speech
• Discography
• Bibliography
• Videos
• Cultural Centers,
Artisans, Networking
• Index

WHERE TO WRITE FOR FURTHER INFORMATION ABOUT THE TRIBES/ NATIONS INCLUDED OR CITED IN THIS COLLECTION

Acoma Tourist Visitors Center
PO Box 309
Acoma NM 87034

Alabama-Coushatta
Rt. 3 Box 640
Livingston TX 77351

Buffalo Bill Historical Center
(Sioux, Blackfeet, Shoshone, Crow, Arapaho)
720 Sheridan Ave.
Cody WY 82414

Cherokee Heritage Center and National Museum
PO Box 515
Tahlequah OK 74465

Haliwa-Saponi Tribe
PO Box 99
Hollister NC 27844

Kiowa Tribe of Oklahoma
PO Box 369
Carnegie OK 73015

Museum of the Plains Indian
Junction of Route 2 and 89
PO Box 400
Browning MT 59417

Museum of the Cherokee Indian
US Highway 441 N.
PO Box 1599
Cherokee NC 28719

Nanticoke Tribe
Nanticoke Tribal Museum
Millsboro DE

Navajo Tribal Museum
PO Box 308
Window Rock AZ 8651

Oglala Lakota College
PO Box 490
Kyle SD 57752

Pascua Yaqui Tribe
7474 South Camino de Oeste
Tucson AZ 85746

Seneca Iroquois National Museum
PO Box 492
Salamanca NY 14779

Three Affiliated Tribes
(Hidatsa-Mandan-Arikira)
PO Box 220
New Town ND 58763

Tigua Cultural Center
122 South Old Pueblo
El Paso TX 79936

White Mountain Apache Cultural Center
PO Box 507
Old Fort Apache AZ 85926

Zuni Museum
PO Box 339
Zuni NM 87327

IF YOU VISIT A RESERVATION

Recognizing the renewed interest in Native American culture, a growing number of Reservations throughout the United States ("Reserves," in Canada) are actively developing tourism offices and cultural centers to promote travel and cultural education. Visiting a reservation and learning first hand from Native Americans is, perhaps, the most rewarding manner in which to study this vibrant culture.

Prior to visiting a reservation, contact the tribal council to determine if the particular reservation is open to visitors. Some reservations are simply residential areas containing family homes and others may be closed to the public during certain ceremonial events. A list of reservations in or near your state may usually be obtained through state tourism offices along with addresses and telephone numbers for tribal contacts. Tribes, such as the Navajo and Hopi, operate full scale tourism offices to better manage tourist activities on tribal lands.

Admission fees may or may not be charged for visits, but fees and restrictions almost always apply to photography, sketching, and recording while on tribal lands. Complete regulations may be obtained from the tribal council in advance or at specially designated booths at reservation entrances. Proper, conservative, clothing is recommended for visits to most reservations. Because of repeated violations of policies and abuses of privileges by tourists, several tribes have begun to severely restrict activities, particularly during important ceremonial dates.

If possible, begin your visit at the tribal cultural center or museum. These facilities serve to provide accurate cultural and historical information about the tribe and related peoples. Personnel at these centers may be able to assist visitors in contacting musicians, craftsmen, etc. who are willing to provide specialized information. A calendar of events may also be obtained from these sources. Bookstores and gifts shops affiliated with the tribal centers offer a wide range of cultural items for sale and may provide contact with individuals who will work on commissioned items.

Respect the homes and businesses on the reservation as you would your own neighborhood. One Navajo remarked, "How would you like for a bunch of us to climb over a fence into your yard, trample your garden, and take pictures through your bedroom window?" Always ask permission before photographing individuals or their property. Some gladly give permission, others will politely refuse, and still others will expect a "gift" of money for the privileges requested.

Respect the beliefs and customs of the Native Americans and be sensitive to comments you make regarding living conditions, clothing, etc. Remember: the way you live may look a bit strange to a visitor from another culture, too. In conversation, avoid stereotypes and cliches regarding Native Americans. A faux pas actually witnessed at the Grand Canyon: As a group of young children escaped from a day's captivity in the family travel trailer, their mother shouted, "Now don't go acting like a bunch of wild Indians!" Imagine the feelings of the numerous Native Americans in the parking lot and store!

Most Native Americans are fiercely proud of their heritage and are eager to help a genuinely interested visitor better understand the culture. Be courteous, be sincere—you'll be gratified by the response.

WE ARE PART OF THE EARTH AND IT IS PART OF US: CHIEF SEATTLE'S SPEECH

(The Native American peoples have always had a deep respect for the environment. Each creature was considered as a Brother to the Human and the Earth itself was viewed as Humankind's Mother. Through balancing the needs of Humanity and the needs of Nature, the Native American created system of environmental management.

In 1854, the Puget Sound Tribe was asked to sell a large tract of land in what is now the State of Washington. The reply by their leader, Chief Seattle, remains one of the most eloquent statements on the environment ever made. Even today, this speech is frequently quoted by those advocating a return to environmental balance.)

"**H**ow can you buy or sell the sky, the warmth of the land? The idea is strange to us. If we do not own the freshness of the air and the sparkle of the water, how can you buy them?

"Every part of the earth is sacred to my people. Every shining pine needle, every sandy shore, every mist in the dark woods, every clearing, and humming insect is holy in the memory and experience of my people. The sap which courses through the trees carries the memories of the red man.

"The white man's dead forgot the country of their birth when they go to walk among the stars. Our dead never forget this beautiful earth, for it is the mother of the red man. We are a part of the earth and it is a part of us. The perfumed flowers are our sisters; the deer, the horse, the great eagle, these are our brothers. The rocky crests, the juices in the meadows, the body heat of the pony, and the man—all belong to the same family.

"So, when the Great Chief in Washington sends us word that he wishes to buy our land, he asks much of us. The Great Chief sends word that he will reserve us a place so that we can live comfortably to ourselves. He will be our father and we will be his children. So we will consider your offer to buy our land, But it will not be easy—this land is sacred to us.

"This shining water that moves in the streams and the river is not just water but the blood of our ancestors. If we sell you our land, you must remember that it is sacred and you must teach your children that it is sacred and that each ghastly reflection in the clear waters of the lakes tells of events and memories in the life of my people. The water's murmur is the voice of my father's father.

"The rivers are our brothers, they quench our thirst. The rivers carry our canoes and feed our children. If we sell you our land, you must remember and you must teach your children that the rivers are our brothers and yours and you must henceforth give the rivers the kindness you would give any brother.

"We know that the white man does not understand our ways. One portion of land is the same to him as another, for he is a stranger who comes in the night and takes from the land whatever he needs. The earth is not his brother but his enemy, and, when he has conquered it, he moves on. He leaves his fathers' graves and children's birthright forgotten. He treats his mother, the earth, and his brother the sky, as things to be bought, plundered, sold like sheep or bright beads. His appetite will devour the earth and leave behind only desert.

"I do not know. Our ways are different from your ways. The sight of your cities pains the eyes of the red man. Perhaps it is because the red man is savage and does not understand.

"There is no quiet place in the white man's cities. No place to hear the unfurling of leaves in the spring, or the rustle of an insect's wings. Perhaps it is because I am savage and do not understand. The clatter only seems to insult the ears. What is there to life is a man cannot hear the lonely cry of the whippoorwill or the arguments of the frogs around a pond at night? I am a red man and do not understand. The Indian prefers the soft sound of the wind darting over the face of a pond and the smell of the wind itself cleansed by a rain or scented with the pine cone.

"The air is precious to the red man for all things share the same breath: the beast, the tree, the man all share the same breath. The white man does not seem to notice the air he breathes. Like a man dying for many days, he is numb to the stench. If we sell you our land, you must remember that the air is precious to us, that the air shares its spirit with all the life it supports. The wind that gave our grandfather his first breath also received his last. If we sell you our land, you must keep it apart and sacred as a place where even the white man can go and taste the wind that is sweetened by the meadow's flowers.

"So we will consider your offer to buy our land. If we decide to accept, I will make one condition: the white man must treat the beasts of this land as his brothers.

"I am savage and do not understand any other way. I have seen a thousand rotting buffaloes on the prairie left by the white man who shot them from a passing train. I am savage and do not understand how the smoking iron horse can be more important than the buffalo that we kill only to stay alive.

"What is man without the beasts? If all the beasts were gone, man would die from a great loneliness of spirit for whatever happens to the beasts also happens to man. All things are connected.

"You must teach your children that the ground beneath their feet is the ashes of our grandfathers. So that they will respect the land, tell your children that the earth is rich with the lives of our kin. Teach your children what we have taught our children, that the earth is our mother. Whatever befalls the earth befalls the sons of the earth. Man did not weave the web of life, he is merely a strand within it. Whatever he does to the web, he does to himself.

"Even the white man whose God walks and talks with him as friend to friend cannot be exempt from the common destiny. We may be brothers after all. We shall see. One thing we know which the white man may one day discover: our God is the same God. You may think that you own Him as you wish to own our land, but you cannot. He is the God of all humanity and his compassion is equal for the red man and the white. The earth is precious to him and to harm the earth is to heap contempt upon its Creator. The whites, too, shall pass—perhaps sooner than all the other tribes. Contaminate your bed and you will one night suffocate in your own waste.

"But, in your perishing, you will shine brightly, fired by the strength of the God who brought you to this land and for some special purpose gave you dominion over this land and over the red man. That destiny is a mystery to us, for we do not understand when the buffalo are slaughtered, the wild horses are tamed, the secret corners of the forest heavy with the scent of many men and the view of the ripe hills blotted out by talking wires.

"Where is the thicket? Gone! Where is the eagle? Gone!"

DISCOGRAPHY

The following discography is formatted quite simply:

- First, the name and address of the recording company *&/or distributor* is listed for convenience in ordering or in obtaining more detailed catalogs.
- Then, a list of recordings available from that source is given showing the record number and key words from the record title. The listed information should prove sufficient to give a guide to contents and to provide minimal information needed to place an order.

SMITHSONIAN/FOLKWAYS
Office of Folklife Programs
955 L'Enfant Plaza, Suite 2600
Smithsonian Institution
Washington, D.C. 20560

Record Number	*Title*
4003	Songs & Dances of the Great Lakes Indians
4069	Eskimo Songs from Alaska
4070	Music of the Alaskan Kutchin Indians
4072	Seneca Social Dance Music
4119	Haida: Indian Music of the Pacific Northwest
4122	Kwakiutl, Northwest Coast Indians (2 records)
4140	Turtle Mountain Music
4251	Healing Songs of the American Indians
4252	Music of the Plains. Apache
4253	Music of the Algonkians
4328	Comanche Flute Music (Doc Tate)
4381	War Whoops and Medicene Songs
4383	Songs of the Florida Seminoles
4384	Washo-Peyote Songs
4392	Chippewa Songs Vol I
4393	Kiowa Songs
4394	Hopi Katcina Songs & Hopi Chanters
4401	Music of the Sioux and Navajo
4420	Music of the American Indians of the Southwest
4444	Eskimos of Hudson Bay and Alaska
4445	Songs and Dances of the Flathead Indians
4464	Indian Music of the Canadian Plains
4523	Indian Music of the Pacific Northwest
4524	Nootka Music. Pacific Northwest. British Columbia
4541	North American and Eskimo Music
4542	Anthology of Central and South American Indians
4601	Kiowa Peyote Meeting. 3 albums
6510	American Indian Dances
8850	Indian Music of the Southwest
34001	Historical Album of Blackfoot Indian Music
37254	The Promised Land. Indian Songs of Lament & Protest
37255	Contemporary American Indian Songs
37777	A Cry From the Earth. Music of North American Indians

This listing contains those items produced by Canyon as well as those produced by numerous other Native American recording specialty companies. The subheadings are those used by Canyon Records.

Record Number   Title

NORTHERN PLAINS

6080	Songs of the Arapaho Sun Dance
6115	White Shield Singers
6091	Cree Pow Wow Songs
8031	Cree Pow Wow Songs #2
6104	Pow Wow Songs from Rocky Boy
6154	Pow Wow Songs from Rocky Boy #2
6105	Flathead Stick Game Songs
6116	Hidatsa Songs
6114	Mandaree Singers
8002	Mandaree Singers #2

BLACKFEET

6095	From the Land of the Blackfeet
6119	Blackfeet Pow Wow Songs
6164	Young Grey Horse Society #1
6184	Young Gray Horse Society #2
6193	Young Gray Horse Society #3
6176	Two Medicine Lake Singers #1
6182	Two Medicine Lake Singers #2
6177	Heart Butte Singers #1
6187	" " " #2
6178	Kicking Woman Singers #1
6181	" " " #2
6183	" " " #3
6200, 1	New Kicking Woman Singers #4, 5
6188	Blackfeet Handgame Songs
6189	Little Corner Singers
6190	Spotted Eagle Singers
6195; 6202-4	Black Lodge Singers # 1, 2,3,4

NORTHWEST STATES

6121	Chemiwai Singers
6196	Chemewa Singers 1987
6124	Stick Game Songs
6174	Bad Canyon Wellpinit Singers
6131	Umatilla Tribal Songs
6123	Songs of the Warm Springs Indian Reservation
6126	Yakima Nation Singer-Satus Longhouse
6129	Songs of the Yakima Encampment
6173	Treaty of 1855 Yakima-Wasco
6125	Songs & Stories From Neah Bay

SIOUX

6059	Sioux Favorites
6062	Songs of the Sioux
6079	Fort Kipp Sioux Singers
6101	" " " " #2
6152	Fort Kipp Celebration
8034	Fort Kipp Singers '77 Live
6081	Sioux Rabbit Songs
6150	Sioux Songs of Love & War
6112	Sisseton-Wahpeton Singers
8066	Porcupine Singers # 1
8007	" " #2
8008	" " #3 NOTE: These singers provided
8010	" " #4 traditional music for the movie
6191	" " #5 "Dances With Wolves"
6192	" " #6
8030	Ironwood Singers
8032	Rock Creek Singers #1
	Sioux/Assiniboine Singers #1
	Sioux Assiniboine Singers #2
	Red Nation Singers Vol 1
	Taku Wakan: Lakota Sunndance Songs

WESTERN CANADA

6132	Blackfoot A-1 Singers #1
9007	Blackfoot A-1 Singers #2
9009	Crowfoot Singers #1
6113	Songs from the Blood Reserve
6134	Treaty 6 Ermine Skin Band (Cree)
6156, 7	The Drums of Poundmaker #1, 2
6163	Pigeon Lake Singers #1
9001	Pigeon Lake Singers #2
6169	Little Pine Singers (Cree)
9005	Two Nation Singers
6130	Songs of the Sarcee
9011	Sarcee Broken Knife Singer Vl 2
6097	Pezhin Wachipi Grass Dance Songs
6136	Stoney Pow Wow Songs
9003	Chiniki Lake Drummers
6142	Songs from the Battleford Pow Wow
9014	Stoney Park Singers
6206	Little Boy Singers
	Red Bull Singers #1, 2
	Elk's Whistle
	Dakota Hotain Singers #1, 2
	Assiniboine, Jr
	Blackstone Cree Pow Wow Songs
	Whitefish Bay Singers #1, 2

MIDWEST/GREAT LAKES

6082	Chippewa War Dance Songs
6106	Chippewa Grass Dance Songs
6170	Kingbird Singers
8013	Songs of the Chippewa

6090	Mesquakie Bear Singers
6171	White Earth Pow Wow
6194	Woodlad Singers (Mesquakie)
	Ojibway Music from Minnesota (Minnesota Historical Society)
RYKO 0199	Honor the Earth Pow-Wow: Songs of the Great Lakes Tribes

SOUTHERN PLAINS: OKLAHOMA

6146, 7	Songs of the Caddo #1, 2
6087	Kiowa 49 and Round Dance Songs
6103	Kiowa Gourd Dance Songs
6145	Kiowa War,49, and Horse Stealing Songs
6148	Gourd Dance Songs of the Kiowa
6166	Kiowa Scalp and Victory Dance Songs
6167	Kiowa Blacklegs Society Songs
6143	Ponca War Dances
6088	Southern Style War Dances
6172	Brave Scout Singers (Otoe & Pawnee)

EASTERN

	Iroquois Social Dance Songs # 1, 2, 3
NW 337	Songs & Dances of Eastern Indians from Medicine Spring (Cherokee) and Allegany (Seneca)
IS 9001	Ceremonial Songs & Dances of the Cherokee

YAQUI

6099	Yaqui Music of the Pascola & Deer Dance
6140	Yaqui Ritual & Festive Music
7998	Yaqui Pascola Music of Arizona
8001	Indian Music of Northwest Mexico

PIMA/PAPAGO

6084	Traditional Papago Music
6098	Papago Dance Songs
6066	Songs from the Pima
	Traditional Pima Dance Songs

UTE

| 6113 | Utes: War, Bear, & Sun Dance Songs |

APACHE

6053	Apache
6165	Songs of the White Mountain Apache
703,4	Remembering Murphy Cassa #1,2
705	Songs of the Arizona Apache

PUEBLO

6072	Hopi Butterfly
6107, 8	Hopi Social Dance Songs #1, 2
6058	Songs from Laguna
6065	Pueblo Songs from San Juan
6060	Zuni Ceremonial Songs

INTERTRIBAL GROUPS

6050	The Song of the Indian
6052	Great Plains Singers & Songs
6110	Bala Sinem Choir: American Indian Songs and Chants
6149	Bala Sinem Choir: Walk in Beauty My Children
6089	Crow Celebration
6096	Denver Indian Singers
6111	Kyi-yo Pow Wow
6122	Northern Plains Society Singers
6175	Omak Pow Wow 1980
6180	Hopi Sunshield Singers
6185,6,7,8,9	White Eagle Singers #1-5
	Santa Fe Pow Wow: 1990

NAVAJO

6160	Natay, Navajo Singer
6057	Memories of Navajoland
6055	Songs of the Dine'
6064	Traditional Navajo Songs
6067	Navajo Squaw Dance Songs
6069	Yei-Be-Chai Songs
6117	Dine' Ba' Aliil of Navajoland
6168	Bita Hochee Travelers Vol 1
8041	" " " Vol 3
8042	Bita Hochee Travelers Vol 4
8044, 45	Four Corners Singers Vol1, 2
8048	" " " ' 3
7143, 44, 45	" " " ' 5, 6, 7
7140	Rock Point Singers Vol 3
7155	" " " ' 4
7126, 27	Chinle Valley Boys Vol 1, 2
7141, 42	" " " ' 3, 4
7125	San Juan Singers
7128, 29, 30	Dennehotso Swinging Wranglers Vol 1, 2, 3
7134, 35	Chinle Valley Singers Vol 1, 2
7137	Toh-Den-nas-Shai Singers
7148, 49	Tsi Yi Tohi Singers Vol 1
7153	" " " " '3
7146	Nanaba Midge Sings Traditional Navajo Songs
7150, 51	Beclabito Valley Singers Vol 3, 4
7152	Four Corners Yei-Be-Chai
7132, 33	Chinle Valley Festival #1, 2
7159	Sweethearts of Navajoland
	Lupton Valley Singers # 1
	Davis Mitchell # 1, 2
	Ned Tsosie Clark
	Chinle Swinging Echoes
	D.J. Nez
	Ned Morris
	Whippoorwill Singers Vol 1

PEYOTE SONGS

6054	Peyote Collection
6068	Chants of the Native American Church
6094	Peyote Healing Chants
6144	Kiowa Peyote Songs
6159	Navajo Wildcat Peak # 1
8014, 15, 16	Navajo Wildcat # 2, 3, 4
8037	" " " #5
8026	Navajo Wildcat Peak Youth
8018,19	Peyote Prayer Songs # 1, 2
8021	Peyote Songs Vol 2
8022, 23, 24	Peyote Songs from Rocky Boy # 1, 2, 3
8025	Lord's Prayer Songs
8027, 28, 29	Intertribal Peyote Chants #1, 2, 3
8035, 36	Intertribal Peyote Chants # 4, 5
	Billie Nez: Peyote Songs from Navajoland

FEATHERSTONE RECORDS (Primarily Northern Plains music; available from Canyon)

FT 1001	Mandan,Hidatsa,Arikira Traditional Songs
FT 1002	Dakota Love Songs
FT 1003	New Town Singers Live at Dakota Dance Clan
FT 1004	Mandaree Singers Live at New Town
FT 1005	Old Scout Singers at White Shield
FT 1006	Wahpe Kute—Live at Dakota Dance Clan
FT 1007	Eagle Whistles Live at Mandaree
FT 1008	The Buckaroos (Ojibway)
FT 1009	Little Earth Singers
FT 1010	Ft Yates Singers
FT 1011	Rock Creek Singers
FT 1012	Mandaree Singers Live at Bismarck
FT 1013	Eagle Whistles Live at Bismarck Vol 2
FT 1014	Assiniboine Singers
FT 1015	Dajota Tipi Live
FT 1016	Red Nation Singers at Ft Totten Days
FS 4001	Kevin locke Lakota Flute # 1
FS 4004	" " " " #2
FS 4002	All Nations Singers—Flandreau School
FS 4003	Songs of the People
FS 4007	Music of the Plains (flute)
FS 4008	Voices of the Earth (flute)

HIGHSTAR PRODUCTIONS (Available from Canyon)

HSP 85-122	Red Leaf Singers
HSP 87-31	Denver March Pow Wow
HSP 87-1201	Eagle Whistles Vol 1
HSP 87-1202	Eagle Whistles Vol 2
HSP 87-71	Red Leaf Takoja
HSP 88-0301	Red Leaf Takoja

CONTEMPORARY (Available from Canyon)

Jim Boyd—Reservation Bound
Arliene Nofchissey Williams—Encircle
Chief Dan George—Proud Earth
The Northern Express—Just Arriving
Frank Monyano—Reservation Reflections

A. Paul Ortega—Two Worlds; Three Worlds
Ortega With Sharon Burch—Blessing Ways
Sharon Burch—Yazzie Girl
Buddy Red Bow—Journey to the Spirit World
Joanne Shenandoah
Gene T—American Indian Music
Billy Thunderkloud—Off the Reservation
John Trudell—AKA Grafitti Man; Tribal Voice; But This Isn't El Salvador
Floyd Westerman—The Land is Your Mother; Custer Died for Your Sins

NATIVE AMERICAN FLUTE (Including "New Age"; available from Canyon)

Andean Music—Ñanda Mañachi
Gordon Bird—Music of the Plains
Fernando Cellicion— Traditional and Contemporary Flute of Fernando Cellicion; Buffalo Spirit
Robert Tree Cody—Traditional Flute Music Vol 1; Lullabies & Traditional Vol. 2;
Herman Edwards—Flute Music of the Okanagan
Daniel C. Hill—Winter Night Song; Waterlands of Turtle Island
Kevin Locke—The Seventh Direction; Make Me a Hollow Reed; Love Songs of the Lakota
Tom Mauchahty-Ware—Flute Songs of the Kiowa and Comanche
Frank Montano—Eternal Journey
R. Carlos Nakai—Changes; Cycles;Journeys;Earth Spirit;Canyon Trilogy; Sundance Season son;
    Desert Dance; Jackalope Vol 1; Jackalope (Weavings)
Larry Yanez—Suenos/Dreams
Nakai with William Eaton—Carry the Gift; Winter Dreams
William Eaton—Tracks We Leave
Nakai with Peter Kate—Natives
Cornel Pewewardy—Flute and Prayer
John Rainer—Songs of the Indian Flute Vol 1 and Vol 2
Rainmaker—Distant Thunder
Stan Snake—Dawn of Love
Douglas Spotted Eagle—Sacred Feelings; Legends of the Flute Boy

CHICKEN SCRATCH—(Popular Dance Music of the Indians of Southern Arizona; available from Canyon)

6085	Mike Enis/Conjunto Murrietta
6093	The Molinas
6109	More Chicken Scratch
6120	The American Indians Vol 1
6138	The Cisco Band Vol 1
6161	The Molinas Vol 3
6162	El Conjunto Murrietta Tocando Norteno
8050	Gila River Six (minus one)
8051	Santan Vol 1
8052	The Blood Brothers Vol 1
8055	Chicken Scratch Fiesta
8056	Santan Vol 2
8057	The Papago Raiders Vol 1
8058	The Cisco Band Vol 2
8059	The Papago Sunliners Vol 1
8060	The Legends
8061	Santan Vol 3
8062	The Santa Rosa Band Vol 2
8063	"Los Papagos" Vol 3
8064	The Papago Raiders vol 2
8065	The Papago Sunliners Vol 2

8066	Verton Jackson Combo
8067	Virgil Jose and Friends
8068	The Blood Brothers Vol 2
8069	Tribesmen
8070	The Papago Raiders Vol 3
8071	The Santa Rosa Band Vol 3
8072	The American Indians Vol 3
8074	The Cisco Band Vol 3
8075	The Papago Indian Band
8076	Papago Express
8077	The Blood Brothers Vol 3
8078	Thee/Express
8079	Tohono O'Odham Braves
8080	Virgil Jose and Friends
8081	Tohono Raiders Vol 4
8082	Gu Achi Fiddlers—Old Time Chicken Scratch
8083	T.O. Combo
8084	The Santa Rosa Band Vol 4
8085	San Xavier Fiddle Band
8086	Tohono O'Odham Braves Vol 2
8087	Los Papagos Molinas Vol 6
8088	Virgil Jose and Friends Vol 3

TRIBAL MUSIC INTERNATIONAL (Available from Canyon)

Music from the Hopi
Music from San Juan Pueblo
Red Eagle Wing Pow Wow Songs
Flute & Prayer Songs (Comanche-Kiowa)
Alliance West Singers (Southern Plains)
65th Gallup Intertribal Ceremonial
Andean Music
Music from Zuni Pueblo

INDIAN SOUNDS RECORDS
PO Box 6038
Moore, Oklahoma 73153

IS 1001, 2, 3,4	Round Dance Songws # 1 English lyrics; 2, 3, 4
IS 2001,2	Pow Wow Songs from Oklahoma # 1, 2
IS 2010,11	The Contest is On! # 1, 2
IS 2501	Kiowa Flag Song
IS 3030,31	Indian Chipmunks Vol 1, 2
IS 4901	Let's 49
IS 4911	Forty-nine songs with English Lyrics
IS 5050	Traditional & Contemporary Indian Flute Music
IS 5051	Sunrise--American Indian Flute (Tom Mauchahty-Ware)
IS 5060	Zuni Indian Flute Music
IS 5061	Fernando Cellicion--Indian Flute
IS 6001	Pow Wow & Specialty Dance Songs form Oklahoma
IS 8001	Navajo Peyote Songs
IS 9001	Cherokee Ceremonial Songs & Dances

IH 1001,2	Round Dance Songs—Taos Pueblo Vol 1, 2
IH 1003, 4	Taos Round Dance Part 1, 2
IH 1005	Taos Pueblo Round Dance
IH 1006, 7	Taos Pueblo Round Dance Songs Vol 1, 2
IH 1051	Ditch Cleaning & Picnic Songs—Picuris Pueblo
IH 1101	Turtle Dance Songs—San Juan Pueblo
IH 1102	Cloud Dance Songs—San Juan Pueblo
IH 1401	Zuni Fair
IH 1501	Navajo Sway Songs
IH 1502	Night & Daylight Yei-Be-Chei
IH 1503	Navajo Skip Dance & Two Step Songs
IH 1504	Navajo Round Dance
IH 1505	Navajo Gift Songs
IH 1507	Navajo Corn Grinding Songs
IH 1508	Klagetoh Maiden Singers
IH 1509-14	Navajo Songs About Love # 1-6
IH 1521	San Juan Singers—Navajo Skip Dance Songs
IH 1523, 4	Turtle Mt Singers—Navajo Social Dance Songs
IH 1531, 2	Rock Point Singers Vol 1, 2
IH 1535	Southern Maiden Singers—Skip and Two Step
IH 1541-4	Navajo Peyote Songs Vol 1-4
IH 2001, 2	War Dances of the Ponca Vol 1, 2
IH 2005,6,7	Ponca Peyote Songs Vol 1, 2, 3
IH 2201,2	Cheyenne Peyote Songs Vol 1, 2
IH 2401,2	Comanche Peyote Songs Vol 1, 2
IH 2501,2	Handgame Songs—Kiowa, Kiowa/Apache,Comanche # 1, 2
IH 2503, 4	Kiowa Gourd Dance Vol 1, 2
IH 2005	Kiowa 49 & War Songs
IH 2506, 7	Kiowa Church Songs Vol 1, 2
IH 2508, 9	War Dance Songs of the Kiowa Vol 1, 2
IH 2512	Flute Songs of the Kiowa & Comanche (Tom Mauchahty-Ware)
IH 3001, 2	Songs of the Muskogee Creek PT 1, 2
IH 3003, 4	Stomp Dance (Muskogee, Seminole, Creek) Vol 1, 2
IH 4001, 2	Blackfoot A-1 Club Singers Vol 1, 2
IH 4003	Blackfoot Crossing
IH 4051, 2	Old Agency Singers of the Blood Reserve Vol 1, 2
IH 4101	The Badlands Singers (Assiniboine & Sioux)
IH 4102	Sounds of the Badlands Singers
IH 4103	Badlands Singers Live at Bismarck
IH 4104	Badlands Singers at Home
IH 4105	Kahomini Songs--Badlands Singers
IH 4106, 7	The Badlands Singers Vol 1, 2
IH 4201	Ashland Singers (Northern Cheyenne War Dance)
IH 4301	Ho Hwo Sju Lakota Singers (Traditional Lakota Sioux)
IH 4315	Love Songs of the Lakota (Kevin Locke)
IH 4321	Ironwood Singers—Songs of the Sioux
IH 4322	Ironwood Singers—Rosebud Sioux Fair
IH 4371-8	Yankton Sioux Peyote Songs Vol 1-8
IH 4379	Songs of the Native American Church
IH 4401	Chippewa-Cree Grass Dance Songs
IH 4501	Red Earth Singers Live at Bismarck

IH 4502	Red Earth Singers
IH 9501	Sounds of Indian America—Plains/Southwest
IH 9502	Pueblo Songs of the Southwest

LYRICHORD INC
141 Perry Street
New York City, NY 10014

7373	Canadian Blackfeet Indian Songs
7379	Eskimos of Greenland and Canada
7380	Eskimos of the Arctic Circle

LIBRARY OF CONGRESS RECORDS
James Madison Building; The Library of Congress
Washington, DC 20540

L-17	Seneca Songs of the Coldspring Longhouse
L-24	Songs of the Yuma, Cocopa, Yaqui
L-25	Songs of the Pawnee & Northern Ute
L-31	Songs of the Papago
L-32	Songs of the Nootka & Quiliute
L-33	Songs of the Menominee, Mandan, and Hidatsa
L-34	Indian Sounds of the Northwest
L-35	Songs of the Kiowa
L-36	Indian Songs of Today
L-38	Songs of the Paiute, Washo, Ute, Bannock, Shoshone
L-39	Comanche, Cheyenne, Kiowa, Caddo, Wichita, Pawnee Songs
L-40	Songs of the Sioux
L-41	Songs of the Navajo
L-42	Songs of the Apache
L-43	Pueblo: Taos, San Ildefonso, Zuni, Hopi
L-71	Omaha Indian Music

BIBLIOGRAPHY

Allen, Paula Gunn. (1986). *The Sacred Hoop*. Boston: Beacon Press.

Anderson, William and Patricia Shehan Campbell. (1989). *Multicultural Perspectives in Music Education*. Reston, Virginia: Music Educators National Conference.

Anderson, William M. (1991). *Teaching Music With a Multicultural Approach*. Reston, VA: Music Educators National Conference.

Bahti, Tom. (1968). *Southwestern Indian Tribes*. Flagstaff, Arizona: KC Publications, Inc.

———. (1970). *Southwestern Indian Ceremonials, 1982 edition*. Flagstaff, Arizona: KC Publications, Inc.

Ballard, Louis W. (1973). *American Indian Music for the Classroom*. Phoenix, Arizona: Canyon Records.

Bierhorst, John. (1985). *The Mythology of North America*. New York: William Morrow.

———. (1979, 1992). *A Cry from the Earth*. Santa Fe, New Mexico: Ancient City Press.

Brown, Dee. (1970). *Bury My Heart at Wounded Knee*. New York: Holt, Rinehart, and Winston.

Brown, Joseph E. (1992). *Animals of the Soul*. New York: Element Books.

Brundin, Judith A. Ed. (1990) *The Native People of the Northeast Woodlands*. New York: Museum of the American Indian–Heye Foundation.

Caduto, Michael J. and Joseph Bruchac. (1988, 1989). *Keepers of the Earth: Native American Stories and Environmental Activities for Children*. Golden, CO: Fulcrum Publishing.

———. (1991). *Keepers of the Animals: Native American Stories and Wildlife Activities for Children*. Golden, CO: Fulcrum Publishing.

Callahan, Alice Anne. (1990). *The Osage Ceremonial Dance I'n-Lon-Schka*. Norman, OK: University of Oklahoma Press.

Campbell, Joseph. (1988). *Historical Atlas of World Mythology*. Vol. I: *The Way of the Animal Powers*; Vol. II: *The Way of the Seeded Earth*. New York: Harper and Row, Inc.

Chazanoff, Daniel. (1990). *Music of the Native North American for the Flute or Recorder*. Brasstown, NC: Susato Press.

Courlander, Harold. (1971). *The Fourth World of the Hopi*. Albuquerque, New Mexico: University of New Mexico Press.

Culin, Stewart. (1902, 1975). *Games of the North American Indians*. New York: Dover.

Curtis, Natalie. (1907, 1987). *The Indians' Book*. New York: Dover Publications.

De Cesare, Ruth. (1988). *Myth, Music and Dance of the American Indian*. Van Nuys: Alfred.

Denig, Edwin Thompson. (1961). *Five Indian Tribes of the Upper Missouri*. Norman, Oklahoma: University of Oklahoma Press.

Densmore, Frances. (1910 and 1913). Chippewa Music Vols. I and II. Washington, D.C.: Bureau of American Ethnology, Bulletin 45 and 53, The Smithsonian Institution.

Dor-Ner, Zui. (1991). *Columbus and the Age of Discovery*. New York: William Morrow.

Dutton, Bertha. (1983). *American Indians of the Southwest*. Albuquerque, New Mexico: University of New Mexico Press.

Edwards, Margot and Ella Clark. (1989). *Voices of the Winds*. New York: Facts on File.

Erdoes, Richard and Alfonso Ortiz. (1984). *American Indian Myths and Legends*. New York: Pantheon Books.

Ewers, John C. (1968). *Indian Life on the Upper Missouri*. Norman, Oklahoma: University of Oklahoma Press.

Fenton, William. (1991). *The Iroquois Eagle Dance.* Syracuse, NY: Syracuse Univ. Press.

Fergusson, Erna. (1931, 1988). *Dancing Gods: Indian Ceremonies of New Mexico and Arizona.* Albuquerque, New Mexico: University of New Mexico Press.

Freedman, Russell. (1987). *Indian Chiefs.* New York: Holiday House.

———. (1992). *An Indian Winter.* (Paintings and Drawings by Karl Bodmer). New York: Holiday House.

Gattuso, John. (1991). *Native America.* Singapore: APA Publications.

George, Luvenia A. (1987) Teaching the Music of Six Different Cultures. Danbury, CT: World Music Press.

Gilpin, Laura. (1968). *The Enduring Navajo.* Austin, Texas: University of Texas Press.

Hart, Mickey and Frederich Liebermann. (1991). *Planet Drum.* New York: Harper Collins.

Hart, Mickey and Jay Stevens. (1990) *Drumming at the Edge of Magic.* San Francisco: Harper Collins.

Harvey, Karen D., Lisa D. Harjo, and Jane K. Jackson. (1990). *Teaching About Native Americans.* Washington, D. C. : National Council for the Social Sciences.

Heth, Charlotte, ed. (1992). *Native American Dance: Ceremonies and Social Traditions.* Washington, DC: National Museum of the American Indian.

Howard, James H. and Victoria Lindsay Levine. (1990). *Choctaw Music and Dance.* Norman, OK: University of Oklahoma Press.

Hoyt-Goldsmith, Diane, photos by Lawrence Migdale. (1990). *Totem Pole.* New York: Holiday House.

———. (1991). *Pueblo Storyteller.* New York: Holiday House.

———. (1993). *Cherokee Summer.* New York: Holiday House.

Kavasch, Barrie. (1979) *Native Harvests: Recipes and Botanicals of the American Indian.* NY: Vintage Books (Random House).

Klah, Hasteen. (1942). *Navajo Creation Myth.* Santa Fe, NM: Museum of Navajo Ceremonial Art.

Kurath, Gertrude P. (1964) *Iroquois Music and Dance.* Scholarly Press.

———. (1970). *Music and Dance of the Tewa Pueblos.* Museum of New Mexico Press.

Laubin, Reginald and Gladys Laubin. (1977). *Indian Dances of North America.* Norman, OK: University of Oklahoma Press.

Lavender, David. (1988). *The Way to the Western Sea.* New York: Anchor Books.

Lowie, Robert H. (1954). *Indians of the Plains.* Lincoln,NE: University of Nebraska Press.

Mails, Thomas E. (1972). *The Mystic Warriors of the Plains.* New York: Mallard Press.

———. (1973). *Dog Soldiers, Bear Men, and Buffalo Women.* Englewood Cliffs, NJ : Prentice-Hall, Inc.

———. (1974). *The People Called Apache.* Englewood Cliffs, NJ: Prentice-Hall, Inc.

———.(1978). *Sundancing at Rosebud and Pine Ridge.* Sioux Falls, SD: The Center for Western Studies.

Matthiessen, Peter. (1991). *In the Spirit of Crazy Horse.* New York: Viking.

Maybury-Lewis, David. (1992). *Millennium: Tribal Wisdom and the Modern World.* New York: Viking.

Mitchell, Frank. (1980). *Navajo Blessingway Singer.* Charlotte Frisbie and David McAllester, eds. Tucson: University of Arizona Press.

Nabakov, Peter, ed. (1991). *Native American Testimony.* New York: Viking.

Newcomb, Franc J. and Gladys A. Reichard. (1975).*Sandpaintings of the Navajo Shooting Chant.* New York: Dover Publications.

Page, Susanne and Jake Page. (1982). *Hopi.* New York: Harry N. Abrams, Inc.

Penny, David W. (1992) *Art of the American Indian Frontier.* Detroit: Detroit Institue of Arts.

Pike, Donald. (1974). ANASAZI: *Ancient People of the Rock.* Palo Alto, CA: American West Publications.

Powers, William K. (1990). *War Dance.* Tucson, AZ: University of Arizona Press.

Roessel, Ruth. (1981). *Women In Navajo Society..* Rough Rock, AZ: Navajo Resource Center.

Scully, Vincent. (1989). *Pueblo: Mountain, Village, Dance.* Chicago: University of Chicago Press.

Skaggs, Jimmy M., Fane Downs, and Winifred Vigness. (1971).*Chronicles of the Yaqui Expedition.* Lubbock, TX: West Texas Museum Association.

Sneve, Virginia Driving Hawk. (1989). *Dancing Teepees: Poems of American Indian Youth.* New York: Holiday House.

Spencer, Katherine. (1957). *An Analysis of Navajo Chantway Myths.* Philadelphia: American Folklore Society.

Spicer, Edward. (1984) *Pascua: A Yaqui Village in Arizona.* Tucson, AZ: University of Arizona Press.

Sturtevant, William C. series editor. *Handbook of the North American Indian.* [Vol. IV: *History of Indian-White Relations* (1988); Vol. VI: *Subarctic* (1981); Vol. VII: *Northwest Coast* (1990); Vol. VIII: *California* (1978); Vol. IX: *Southwest* (1979); Vol. X: *Southwest* ·1983); Vol. XI: *Great Basin* (1986); Vol. XV: *Northeast* (1978)] Washington, DC: Smithsonian Institution.

Supplee, Charles, Douglas Anderson, and Barbara Anderson. (1971). *Canyon de Chelly.* Las Vegas, Nevada: KC Publications.

Sweet, Jill. (1985). *Dances of the Tewa Pueblo Indians.* Santa Fe, New Mexico: School of American Research Press.

Taylor, Colin, ed. (1991) *The Native Americans.* New York: Smithmark Press.

Titon, Jeff Todd, General Editor; James T. Koetting, David P. McAllester, David Reck, Mark Slobin. (1984). *Worlds of Music: An Introduction to the Music of the World's Peoples.* New York: Shirmer Books.

Waldman, Carl and Molly Braun. (1985) *Atlas of the North American Indian.* New York: Facts on File.

Walters, Anna Lee. (1989) *The Spirit of Native America: Beauty and Mysticism in American Indian Art.* San Francisco: Chronicle Books.

Weatherford, Jack. (1988). *Indian Givers.* New York:Fawcett Columbus.

———— (1991). *Native Roots.* New York: Crown Publications.

VIDEOS

Beyond Tradition: Contemporary Indian Art and Its Evolution
   More than three hundred examples of prehistoric, historic and contemporary American Indian art presented against a backdrop of flute music in this award-winning video. Printed index to the art and artists is enclosed. 45 minutes, color. Available from Canyon and elsewhere.

The Dennis Alley Wisdom Dancers
   Filmed at the Grand Canyon, the Dennis Alley family offers eight dances, including Women's Fancy Shawl dance, hoop, eagle and war dances, Northern traditional dance, rendition of "Go My Son" (with signs) at a pow-wow. Approximately 30 minutes, color.

Finding the Circle: The American Indian Dance Theater (PBS "Great Performances")
   This video contains a sampling of well-performed songs and dances from tribes throughout the U.S. Performers are members of the American Indian Dance Theatre troupe. Each dance is performed in authentic costume; voice-over narration includes cultural background information on most of the performances, on the significance of the regalia, preparing for a pow-wow, and the importance of dance and music in the lives of the performers. Some of the dances are performed on a stage, some outdoors at pow-wows. Includes flute music, drum duel, round dance, hoop dance, fancy dances, women's dances, pow-wow scenes. 1 hour, color.

The Hopi
   Scenes of family life, work and rituals blend with the sights and sounds of this thousand-year-old culture in northern Arizona. 15 minutes, color. Museum of Northern Arizona.

Into the Circle: An Introduction into Oklahoma Pow-wows and Celebrations
   Features excerpts of dances across Oklahoma. Available from Written Heritage, 8009 Wales St., New Orleans, LA 70126.

Live and Remember
   An in-depth exploration of Lakota sacred traditions as portrayed through song and dance, oral traditions, living today, medicine and the spirit world. Opens with a Sweat Lodge Ceremony, and continues with contributions from the Ironwood Singers, Kevin Locke and others, including Hoop and Eagle dances. 29 minutes, color. Available from Canyon and elsewhere.

More than Bows and Arrows
   Documents the contributions of Native Americans to the development of the United States and Canada. Narrated by N. Scott Momaday. Winner of over eleven awards, recommended by the NEA. 60 minutes, color.

The Navajo
   Family life, history, role of women in religious, social and cultural life. 15 minutes, color. Museum of Northern Arizona.

Songs of Indian Territory: Native American Musical Traditions of Oklahoma.
A sampler of Oklahoma tribes. Part of the Native American Master Artist video series, (T-104).

Teaching the Music of Native Americans
Primarily lectures filmed during the Music Educators National Conference "Multicultural Music Symposium" of April 1990. Features ethnomusicologists and music educators including Ed Schupman and David McAllester. Available from MENC, 1902 Association Dr., Reston VA 22091-1597.

Thunder in the Dells
Spirit of the Hochungra, the Winnebago people of Wisconsin, in dance and history. Available from Ootek Productions, S12229 Round River Trail, Spring Green, Wisconsin 53588, or Canyon.

PBS SERIES:
Six hour-long documentaries on different issues facing contemporary Native Americans, as well as featuring in-depth examinations of individual cultures. Titles include *Winds of Change: A Matter of Promises, Winds of Change: A Matter of Choice, Myths and Moundbuilders, Geronimo and the Apache Resistance, The Spirit of Crazy Horse, Seasons of the Navajo.*

CULTURAL CENTERS, ARTISANS, SUPPLY SHOPS, NETWORKING

(Those listed below are accessible to the ordinary buyer, are aware they are being included here, can provide services or items within a reasonable time frame, and are not extremely expensive. There are many other master instrument makers who prefer not to deal directly with the public, cater to a select audience, or are backed up with orders to 3,000 AD!)

AKWESASNE NOTES

Mohawk Nation via Rooseveltown, NY 13683

National newspaper published by the Mohawk Nation at Akwesasne. Articles deal with issues of interest to tribes from both North and South America. Calendar highlights goings-on all over the country.

AMERICANA INDIAN SHOWS

6616 Columbine Rd.
Flagstaff AZ 86004
(602) 526-9232

This business purchases Native American items from native artisans and sells these materials at very reasonable prices during sales tours throughout the country. The entourage will include one or more Native American artists, jewelry repairmen/makers, and skilled appraisers in addition to a very knowledgeable sales staff. Call or write to be placed on a mailing list notifying you of upcoming show/sales tours in your area.

BLACK CROW

116 Ives St.
Providence RI 02906
(401) 351-3472
Native American crafts, jewelry, prints, books and music.

PHILLIP CARTER, FLUTE MAKER

1706 Pamela Circle
Norman OK 73071
(405) 321-2377

CANYON RECORDS AND INDIAN ARTS

4143 North 16th Street
Phoenix AZ 85016
(602) 266-4823

If it is Native American music and has been recorded, the folks at Canyon Records either have it in stock or can get it for you. Canyon also has a large selection of books and craft supplies although they are not listed in a catalog.

Recently, Canyon has begun stocking instruments at their Phoenix store—peyote rattles, Hopi gourd rattles, flutes, dance sticks, etc. Prices are extremely reasonable. Ask for their fully annotated record and tape catalog.

THE CENTER OF NATIVE ART

Rt. 1
Woolrich ME 04579
(207) 442-8399

DREAMCATCHER

4059 Skippack Pike
Skippack PA 19474

This is a tiny store with ever-changing stock at extremely reasonable prices. Educational programs, lectures, performances, demonstrations sponsored by the store are on-going.

EAGLE WING PRESS
Dept. C, PO Box 579MO
Naugatuck CT 06770
(203) 729-0035
Publishes a journal that focuses on American Indian concerns, a pow-wow and other events calendar, and "Trading Post" listings.

HEARD MUSEUM
22 E. Monte Vista Rd.
Phoenix AZ 85004

HOPI OFFICE OF PUBLIC RELATIONS
Box 123
Kykotsmovi, Arizona 86039
(602) 734-2441
This office can put you in contact with the Hopi Arts and Crafts Guild, the Hopi Cultural Center, and individual craftspersons on the Hopi Reservation (They prefer "Hopiland"). Kachinas, rattles, unbelievable silver jewelry, etc.

HOUSE OF MUSICAL TRADITIONS
7040 Carroll Ave
Takoma Park, Maryland 20912
(301) 270-9090
Not only instruments from Native American culture, but instruments, recordings, and books from literally every conceivable corner of the world. Write or call for catalog.

INDIAN PUEBLO CULTURAL CENTER
2401 12th Street NW
Albuquerque, New Mexico 87102
(800) 288-0721
IPCC is owned and operated by the nineteen pueblos of New Mexico with the gift shops serving as an outlet for artisans and craftsmen of the various pueblos. A large selection of flutes (including cane and cedar) ranging in price from $50 to $500 is usually available in a variety of designs. Drums from Cochiti Pueblo and the more familiar "Taos" drums are available in sizes from toy to table. Rattles of every description are usually in stock. Experts—often the maker of the instrument—are available to help you select. They also serve as a clearinghouse for many "nameless" masters who prefer not to deal directly with the public. In addition, clothing, kachinas, sandpaintings, jewelry, sculpture, rugs—anything Native American—may be found at this source.

THE INDIAN CRAFT SHOP
1050 Wisconsin Ave NW
Washington, D.C. 20007
Somehow connected with the Department of the Interior. Items are authentic and of exceptional quality. Drums, rattles, and flutes periodically show up in stock. The staff can also put you in touch with instrument makers.

INSTITUTE FOR AMERICAN INDIAN STUDIES
Curtis Rd.
Washington, CT 06793
(203) 868-0518
An educational center, museum, art gallery, lifeways demonstration center and bookshop with an ever-changing calendar of events, including visits by musicians, artists, educators.

IROQRAFTS
RR 7P
Ohsweken, Ontario NOA IMO
Canada
One of the best sources for Native American products including bone rattles, hand drums, recordings etc. Tribes of the Iroquois Confederation are best represented.

KAY MOON DREAMER, RATTLE MAKER

RR1 Box N79
Newville WV 26601
(304) 765-7922
Custom order specialities. Fine rawhide rattles with deer antler handles are art quality; very reasonably priced.

MICMAC ASSOCIATION OF CULTURAL STUDIES

Box 961
Sydney, Nova Scotia BIP 6J4
Canada
Publications and crafts regarding Micmac Indians—one of largest groups in Maritime Provinces and Northeastern U.S.

NATIONAL MUSEUM OF THE AMERICAN INDIAN

Smithsonian Institution
3753 Broadway at 155th St.
New York, NY 10032
(212) 283-2420
Art collections spanning more than 10,000 years of Northern and Southern Hemisphere Native American life. Public programs, films, lectures, school programs by arrangement. (The museum will move in late 1994 to The Custom House, 1 Bowling Green, New York NY 10004, and also will be re-named the George Gustav Heye Center, so be sure to call ahead.)

NAVAJO ARTS AND CRAFTS ENTERPRISES

Drawer A
Window Rock, Arizona 86515
(602) 871-4090
Operated by the Navajo Nation, it serves as both clearing house and quality control for Navajo-related materials.

NAVAJO COMMUNITY COLLEGE PRESS

Navajo Community College
Tsaile, Arizona
(602) 724-3311
Publishes numerous titles related to Native American studies including a few on music and dance.

OB ENTERPRISES

3330 E. 66
Gallup, New Mexico 87301
(505) 722-4431
This is a long established trading post featuring Navajo, Hopi, and Zuni items including drums and rattles in addition to the zillions of jewelry, carvings, sandpaintings, etc. sold at wholesale prices. A Navajo "paho" sold for a mere $11 and a small Zuni fetish pot was available for only $12. Store prices average 50% below East Coast prices for Native Americana. Many of the sales clerks are quite knowledgeable and can assist you in selecting merchandise or contacting artisans directly.

DAVE POWELL, FLUTE MAKER

c/o Canyon Records
4143 North 16th St.
Phoenix AZ 85016
(602) 266-4823
Good quality, inexpensive, undecorated and basic flutes.

CHESLEY GOSEYUN WILSON

333 S. Alvernon #60
Tucson, AZ 85711
Master of the art of Apache violin making.

QUALLA ARTS AND CRAFTS MUTUAL INC.
PO Box 310
Cherokee NC 28719
(704) 497-3103
Arts and crafts source for the Cherokee Nation. A catalog is available for $2.00.

THE RESERVATION
PO Box 17706
San Antonio TX 78217
The Reservation has shops in North Star Mall and the River Center on the Riverwalk between the Convention Center and the Alamo. Much of the inventory is jewelry related items, but drums are always in stock, rattles usually in stock, and occasionally a fine flute is available.

ARNOLD RICHARDSON, FLUTE AND DRUM MAKER
PO Box 130
Hollister, NC 27844
A familiar sight at East Coast pow-wows—an excellent flute and drum maker. Be patient if you order through him—he takes his time to get everything "just right."

TROY RICHARDSON, DRUM MAKER
227 Quince St.
Philadelphia, PA 19107
(215) 829-1549
Good quality, reasonable prices, young craftsman.

JOHN RUNNING: PHOTOGRAPHER
PO Box 1237
Flagstaff AZ 86002
Phone: (602) 774-2923 FAX: (602) 774-9079
Extensive archive of outstanding stock photographs/slides of many subjects, including Native Americans in scenes of daily life, powwos, artists at work, children and elders, and more.

SOUTHERN PLAINS INDIAN MUSEUM AND CRAFTS CENTER
PO Box 749
Anadarko OK 73005

STEVE EAGLE'S
Box 88142
Colorado Springs CO 80908
(719) 495-0897
This business provides everything to make dance regalia, Indian crafts, headdresses, etc. Also, ready made items are available including drums, whistles, and clothing. Craft kits include rattles as well as costume and jewelry items. A very thorough catalog is available.

TAOS DRUM COMPANY
PO Box 1916
Taos NM 87571
(505) 758-DRUM
The name of the company speaks for itself. Drums of all sizes, traditionally made.

ZUNI CRAFTSMEN COOPERATIVE ASSOCIATION
Box 426
Zuni, New Mexico 87327
Primarily jewelry, but the catalog is worth drooling over. Occasionally, items can be commissioned.

INDEX

A

Accompaniment, 24
Acoma, 69
Alaska, 27
American Indian Dance Theatre, 108, 109
American Revolution, 9
Apache, 21, 25, 29, 51, 52
Arikira, 98
Authenticity, 21

B

Basket Dance, 70
Bear Dance, 29, 60
Bells, 29, 24, 25
Bibliography, 155
"Bird", 89, 92
Buffalo, 96
Bull roarer, 29

C

Caddo, 16
Cellición, Fernando, 92
Cherokee, 16, 18
    alphabet, 18
Chickasaw, 18
Chief Seattle, 142-143
Chippewa, 31
Choctaw, 16, 18
Circle, dances, 61
    importance of, 17
Cities of Cibola, 94
Civil War, 18
Columbus, 9
Comanche, 31
Coronado, 94
Courting songs, 22
Creek, 18
Crow, 10
Culture areas, 21, 24-25
    California, 25
    Eastern Woodlands, 24, 55
    Great Basin, 24

Northwest Coast, 25, 27
Plains, 24
Southwest, 25, 94, 109, 136
Curtis, Natalie, 114

D

Dances,
    Basket Dance, 71
    Bear Dance, 60
    Eagle Dance, 37
    Fancy Shawl Dance, 37
    Forty-Niner, 37, 38, 61, 77
    Grand Entry, 36
    Grass Dance, 37
    Hoop Dance, 37
    Intertribal, 66-68, 77,
    Jingle Dance, 37
    Pottery Dance, 69
    Rabbit Dance, 77, 82, 83, 103
    Round Dance, 65, 67, 102,
    Shawl Dance (see Nanticoke Shawl Dance)
    Two-Step, 38, 67, 77-80, 84, 85
Dakota, 97
Deer Dance, 29, 104-105
Discography, 145
Drumming, 27
Drums, 24, 25, 26, 27, 134-137
    construction of, 26-27, 28
    hand drum, 27, 137
    log drum, 26, 135
    materials for constructing, 26, 27
    water drum, 27, 136
Drum beater, 27
"Drum," The, 24, 27

F

Fiddle, Apache, 25, 26
Flute, 31, 91-93, 96, 97, 106, 114
Flute songs, 87-98
    Call to Sunrise, 95
    Courting Song, 96

Hidatsa Dance Song, 98
Kiowa Love Song, 97
Pueblo Sunrise Song, 94
Four Directions, 49, 73
"Song to the Four Directions," 43, 48
Fusion, 92, 106

G
Ghost Dance, 61, 113, 115
Ghost Dance Religion, 115

Haliwa-Saponi, 54-56
Harvest dances, 71
Hilliard, Qunicy, 113, 114
Hidatsa, 98
Honoring, 22, 36, 37
Hopi, 69, 108

I
"I Walk in Beauty," 50
Improvisation, 92, 93
Indian Territory, 18
Indios, 9
Instruments,
    traditional, 161-164, 24-25, 26-31,
    (see individual instruments)
    making instruments, 117-137
Intertribal, 21,37, 67
Iroquois, 24, 77, 83
Iroquois Confederacy, 83

J
Jackalope, 106-107
Jazz, 106, 107
Jingles, 29

K
Kiowa, 24, 31, 96
Kokopelli, 31

L
Lakota, 24, 31, 97, 102-104
Languages, 21, 111, 102
    pronunciation of, 45, 46
Legends, 58, 89, 90, 91,
Locke, Kevin, 93

Lumbee, 73
Lyrics, 44

M
Mahooty, Chester, 108
Mandan, 98
Mohawk, 27
Movies, traditional performances in, 102, 106
Music,
    characteristics of, 24-25
    function of, 22

N
Nakai, R. Carlos, 92, 106-07
Nakota, 24
Nanticoke, 73-76
"Native Americans," 9, 10
Navajo, 21, 23, 25, 27, 51
Notation, musical, 15, 45

O
Oklahoma, 96
Onondaga, 27
One-Eyed Ford, 84, 85
Oral tradition, 15, 18, 46
Ornamentation,
    flute, 92, 93

P
Parker,Quanah, 17
Pascola, 104-105
Pemmican, 115
Percussion, 26, 27, 29
Pine Ridge Reservation, 97
Plains, 24, 27, 31, 67, 96, 97
Porcupine Singers, 102
Pow-wow, 35-36, 67,
    guidelines for attending, 38-39,
    origin, 35
Pueblo, 10, 25, 65, 71, 77, 94

R
Rasps, 29, 132-133
Rattles, 24, 25, 28, 29
    gourd, 29
    kachina rattle, 29

turtle shell, 29
wood, 29
Regalia, 22, 36, 37, 38
Religion, 21
Reservation,
    Pine Ridge, Rosebud, 97
    Standing Rock Reservation, 97
    visiting, 141

S

Scrapers, 29
Seminole, 18
Seneca, 23, 27, 83, 84
Sequoyah, 18
Sioux, 11, 24, 133
Songs, 43
    animal, 22
    courting, 22
    games, 22
    honoring, 22
    origins of, 22, 23
    ownership of, 22
    property, 22
    sunrise, 95, 108
    types of, 22
    work songs, 22
Singing, styles, 24-25
Social dances, 85
Spanish, 94, 104, 105
Sun, 108
Symphonic band works, 113
    Ghost Dance, 113-115
Synthesizer, 107, 112
"SynthacousticpunkarachiNavajazz," 106

T

Tarahumara, 27, 132
Tatanka-Ptecila (Short Bull), 113, 114, 115
Tate, Doc, 92
Tejas, 16
Television, traditional music on, 108, 109,
Terminology, 10
Thanksgiving, 71
Tigua, 77
"Trail of Tears," 16, 18
Tribe, 21

"Tumbling strain," 24

U

Ute, 24, 133

V

Variants, 46
Videos, 159
Violin, 25, 26, 105
Vocables, 15, 23, 44,45, 111, 103
Vocal:
    "growling," 24, 25
    range, 24, 25
    shake, 24
    style, 24, 25
    timbre, 24, 25
    "tumbling strain," 24, 25

W

Water drums, 27, 136
Whistles, 25, 26
Wild West Shows, 35
Women, 22, 36, 37,
Wounded Knee, 114, 115
Wovoka, 114, 115

X

XIT, 110-111

Y

Yaqui, 26, 104-105, 132,
Yoeme, see Yaqui

Z

Zuni, 25, 68, 69, 93, 94, 108-109
Zuni Rainbow Dancers, 108

A SELECTION
OF NATIVE
AMERICAN
DESIGNS
FROM THE
SOUTHWEST
FOR USE IN
CREATIVE
PROJECTS

THERE'S MORE WHERE THIS CAME FROM!

If you have enjoyed *Moving Within the Circle: Contemporary Native American Music and Dance,* you will enjoy our other in-depth yet accessible book- and-tape sets of music from around the world. Most take a long look at one culture in particular, include lots of photos, musical transcriptions, cultural background information and a companion tape of every song or piece included in the book. The companion tapes feature performances by musicians from the culture highlighted in almost all cases. All are appropriate for all grade levels and college Introduction to World Music courses.

Silent Temples, Songful Hearts: Traditional Music of Cambodia by Sam-Ang Sam and Patricia Shehan Campbell (American Folklife Center Award Winner)

From Rice Paddies and Temple Yards: Traditional Music of Vietnam by Phong Nguyen and Patrician Shehan Campbell (American Folklife Center Award Winner)

Let Your Voice Be Heard! Songs from Ghana and Zimbabwe by Abraham Kobina Adzenyah, Dumisani Maraire and Judith Cook Tucker

La-Li-Luo Dance Songs of the Chuxiong Yi, Yunnan Province, China by Alan Thrasher (Not appropriate for the lower grades.)

Los Mariachis! An Introduction to the Mariachi Tradition of Mexico by Patricia Harpole and Mark Fogelquist (director of El Mariachi Uclatlan)

Songs and Stories from Uganda by Moses Serwadda, illustrated by Leo and Diane Dillon

The Lion's Roar: Chinese Luogu Percussion Ensembles (Complete Set includes book, audio tape, color slides)
by Han Kuo-Huang and Patricia Shehan Campbell

World Music: A Source Book for Teaching by Lynne Jessup (an annotated bibliography).

New titles always in preparation!
Send for our catalog or order from your favorite dealer.
World Music Press PO Box 2565 Danbury CT 06813-2565